AuthorHouse™
1663 Liberty Drive
Bloomington, IN 47403
www.authorhouse.com
Phone: 1-800-839-8640

First published by AuthorHouse   06/01/2011

ISBN: 978-1-4567-5689-5 (sc)
ISBN: 978-1-4567-5688-8 (dj)
ISBN: 978-1-4567-5687-1 (ebk)

Library of Congress Control Number: 2011904819

Printed in the United States of America

Any people depicted in stock imagery provided by Thinkstock are models, and such images are being used for illustrative purposes only.
Certain stock imagery © Thinkstock.

This book is printed on acid-free paper.

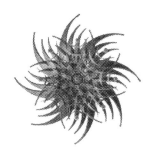

Star

to Star

A Universal Perspective of Life

~ Our universe is simply one blastocyst in Gods universal body. We are merely beings of light and energy that process his energy, by transforming thoughts and ideas into the motions that create life. Unity is not only global, it is universal.

~ The Yin and Yang of life may pull us east and west. But, the destination is always North in the long and winding trail, South takes us against our grain. Create positive thoughts in the morning each day before you venture out into the path of life. Only our path and thoughts, define the journey in the end. Our Universe was started, and can end in a blink of an eye. The good thing is, a blink of an eye relative to size, takes billions of years. But that doesn't mean we should waste the time we have to experience our physical reality arguing over personal perspectives. A thought to keep in mind, with ignorance in hand, people find a happy attitude and a poor perspective, a joyful quest in life. Only with the proper perspectives and morals within our ego can we find the truth in a beneficial and positively progressive direction for everyone.

~ This book may seem a little repetitive at times in its perspective. But realistically, that's how joy and happiness in life are created. Our perspective and attitudes form the way we perceive life and make our decisions, we must think and act repeatedly in a positive direction to accomplish beneficial results. We cannot just tread water in life; we must swim for the shore whenever we can. So bear with me, as with life, the benefit comes with understanding the knowledge, and completing the journey.

The harmony and Unity within our reality, (*God, Brahman, Tao, Spiritualism,+/- Energy, Light/shadow/Dark, Vibrations and Frequencies*). These are related to all major world religions and sciences. They all have a common moral foundation. '*Do unto others as to thyself*'. This is a good idea but an incomplete attempt at peace and unity. It assumes all men have the same morals and feelings of self-worth, we should But we don't. *My quote would be.*

Respect and admire others, then Goodwill and Compassion, will fall upon you.

~ Everyone has their own Perspective and Beliefs. Thus, they should form their own truths. Just remember that the common physical reality doesn't care what you think, only what you act on. Act for life and not strife.

<u>*Familiar Realistic Questions:*</u>
Do all realities exist simultaneously?   Where do we come from? Is there a possibility that all potentials exist side by side? How many dimensions are there really? Why are we here? Who are we? Do our thoughts affect our reality?   Can freewill affect the semi-mechanical chaotic world?   Does GOD exist? And who or what is he?

Some of these questions we can answer through Science, Philosophy, Truth and Logic. All of which you are going to have to look at from an educated perspective, and come to your own conclusions and belief. The benefit of learning should simplify your life as well as the life of others that exist around you. In order to better understand the universe and humanity we live in, you must first realize that we all cause an effect on it, and that we are all affected by it, as well as the others within it. Thus, we can all cause change within it. So, remember as you journey through life, positive actions will generally create positive effects, and negative actions, will cause negative effects for everyone.

Ignorance more frequently begets confidence than does knowledge: it is those who know little, not those who know much, who so positively assert that this or that problem will never be solved by science. (Charles Darwin, Introduction to The Descent of Man, 1871)

Why do we keep recreating the same reality? Why do we keep getting into the same relationships? Why do we keep getting the same jobs? How come we keep recreating the same environments in our infinite sea of endless possibilities that surround us every day? Is it possible that we are so programmed and conditioned by society to our daily life that we believe the illusion that we have no control of our life, and everything is predetermined? I don't believe so. Most have only experienced reality as the perceived world is more real than the internal world, because we can see and touch it. We are all observers living in a universe where we only see the valley of our goals, ignoring the beauty of the mountain tops and the clouds in the sky. We often focus on what is directly in front of us, concentrating our thoughts and efforts on what we know and are familiar with.

The infinite individual actions that are constantly occurring around us are dismissed most of the time. Because, they don't concern us, or because our brain only acknowledges what is happening in our personal view, it takes our spiritual mind to make the decisions that affect our environments and paths. This is really a rather limited direction and percentage of our entire reality. Most people only concern themselves with 15%-20% of their personal environments. This is because that's all we can see from our centred vision. We have peripheral vision that warns of new motion, but the awareness of that is relevant to individual attention.

The actions around us cause us to think and react in the way we have been taught too, most of the time without thought of consequence and based on emotion or ego. Yin or Yang the energy, all our thoughts cause an effect personally and universally, by our thoughts vibrations. Thoughts travel through space instantaneously, mostly affecting those in their relative environment. But they are all ripples in space and time, within a pool of consciousness, eventually to be felt down the line at some time by someone else.

A perfect example of this is the experiments done by Mr. Emoto, and The Messages from Water. These as well as the experiments done that show micro-organisms react instantaneously to the suns solar flares. Shows the unified consciousness exists in everything everywhere. (More information on this later on in the book.)

Within the infinite frequencies of life, there are many variables. The positive and negative energies have a frequency all of their own. This is why we can tell when someone is in a bad mood without having to ask. In life we carry our perspectives and attitude as a torch for others to see.

The base of this flame is found within our conscious mind. This is shown in previous experiments and analysis, relative to our thoughts, choices, and actions. Quantum mechanics and karma are one and the same considering the effect of positive or negative energy. If the attitudes we live with can, and does affect the water that we drink, and surround our self with. Then are we not polluting ourselves by having a poor attitude?

Energy of whatever type electrical or physical Matter can only transform. This may take some time for deterioration with physical Matter, but eventually, even Iron and Rock disintegrate to cycle through the living geological cycle again. This process occurs on such a scale that even the tectonic plates that form our continents and ocean floors, are recycled and regenerated by the volcanic system, and mantle of the planet. This is why the continents move, mountains form, and islands are made. Could it be that our attitude controls our perspective and health? And, that the negative effect can, not only make us sick, but affect our neighbors as well? Could it be that a positive attitude only meets resistance at the hands of the ignorant and arrogant? Or, is it that negative people feel they need to bring others down to their level rather than picking themselves up from a position of discontent.

All our actions have reactions. This is because of the effect of transforming energy. Yin or yang our emotions, It is the Positive or negative actions that cause a positive or negative effect in our current time of reality. If water is our buffer, or shall we say, the oil of our spiritual motor, then as we pollute the water with our negative thoughts, so do we pollute our own journey, this makes our task that much more difficult, and most likely, our children will have to clean up the mess. Think of our universe as a cell in our body. Oxygen-o2 is transferred through the cell membranes and converted to energy, the energy is used and transformed, and then the rest is expelled back through the cell membrane as waste, or Co2. Life and Matter forms and grows depending on our structure's needs. We are one of many structures within many galaxies, yet we are still part of one universe. We are all conscious beings within, and of our own creation.

A reality of realities, we are all made from, and have a common consciousness in our thoughts. One of survival, a wish for peaceful existence without drama, or the discontentment encountered from others, or ourselves, this includes a quest for knowledge and understanding. The basic feelings we all have of Sadness, Joy, Compassion, Love, Anger, Jealousy, and Revenge.

These are all natural but controllable emotions. Due to our personal perspectives and beliefs, society will never accept the truth of reality as a whole until we understand it as individuals. Therefore, we must all realize where we fit into the universe before we can effectively change the environment that influences humanities greed, competitiveness, and self-destructive nature. Hopefully when we get over ourselves, we can look towards the unity, and common good of all creatures and creations. Then we will be consciously connected to the universe, not just physically existing in it. At which time, I believe the universe will become a truly wondrous and beautiful place full of new possibilities.

- *We may agree, perhaps, to understand by Metaphysics an attempt to know reality as against mere appearance, or the study of first principles or ultimate truths, or again the effort to comprehend the universe, not simply piecemeal or by fragments, but somehow as a whole. (Bradley, 1846-1924)*

- *The task is not so much to see what no one yet has seen, but to think what no body yet has thought about that which everyone sees. But life is short, and truth works far and lives long: let us speak the truth. (Arthur Schopenhauer, 1818)*

The first philosophy (Metaphysics) is universal and is exclusively concerned with primary substance. And here we will have the science to study that which is just as that which is, both in its essence and in the properties which, just as a thing that is, it has. The entire preoccupation of the physicist is with things that contain within themselves a principle of movement and rest. And to seek for this is to seek for the second kind of principle, that from which comes the beginning of the change. (Aristotle, Metaphysics, 340BC)

An attempt to know reality as against mere appearance, or the study of first principles or ultimate truths, or again the effort to comprehend the universe, not simply piecemeal or by fragments, but somehow as a whole. (Bradley, 1846-1924)

Recently I have found a certain scientific truth in the interconnection between our physical existence and conscious reality. This being thought and energy, and it has given me a new understanding of our existence and life's purpose. Contrary to what seems to be the majority of social opinion at this point in time, it is the experience of a limited journey through time, in a school of individual, yet universally collective thoughts that form our reality.

This experience should really be enjoyed by the student of life at all times, yet the tides of our age, emotions, and indifference of belief or opinion, form due to our personal perspectives. These thoughts impede our causes and actions, by the effecting our emotions and drawing from our personal desires.

The key to happiness and proper attitude is found in our personal perspective, and how you perceive the path of life's journey. This only you can adjust, compassion shown to another person is reflected back at you through karma and society. The real battle is with ourselves, when we can admit our own faults; we can solve the issues that affect our destination effectively, and not arrogantly. By understanding the nature of Matter and creation, we can logically understand the connection between things that exist in our environment. From this knowledge of a continuous connection, we can solve the problems of humanity with Honesty, Compassion, Physics, Logic, Mathematics, Philosophy, Metaphysics, and Theology in hand. We can do this and keep our equal right to believe in our individual Religions.

Evolution and ecology are constantly advancing our practical applications in science and health. We have, and will progress relevant to the speed at which we can discover ourselves. Beneficial steps towards the progress of humanity and our future are continuously being made, but at times it seems that the right hand, does not keep the left up to date. This may, or may not, be an intentional lack of control, but it is thoughtless, and slows humanities' progress no matter the cause. We should all work as a team and pass the ball around so that everyone can enjoy the game, if you know what I mean. People are free individuals with the freewill of choice, and determination at their grasp. If we can work together by choice, and correct our past errors of human arrogance in our society, then this will ultimately contribute to a better future for humanity by changing our attitude towards life.

The knowledge of our interconnected unity, and the living universe around us, provides us the knowledge and foundation for improving the ecology and life on Earth. Our preservation of nature is critical for our future and survival. By knowing our true nature, we realize that we are a part of nature, and the ecology of life on earth. We can then realize how important it is, to reverse our current destruction of nature and our living environments. This is effectively destroying us and our future. The duality of emotional influence and personal perspective that lie within our path during the journey is something that we all face. This is called life. If we keep a positive perspective within or mind, then we can find the path enlightening along the way. The energy of our conscious thought can be applied in many ways. Memories and past experiences are just a couple; time carries on while you are in thought, no matter where your head is, your body is a reflection of reality. Time is the frequency of energy waves within our life that creates our physical reality. The key is to enjoy not only the moment but, the journey of life during the time you have as well.

Theoretical Metaphysics

Objective experience is about stuff, (what we do, touch, smell). Subjective experience is about the experience. Some scientists believe that the subjective is the purpose. Why we do it, who we are, (the person inside). Some believe that the subjective is real and not the objective, both are actually true. The choices we have and create, define what we do and who we are. By the transmissions of our feelings and senses, we form new thoughts of energy. Then our perspective forms a choice from the options that appear to be at hand. And then, we pass a thought through our bodies to form an action that affects our situations. We cause physical motion only by acting on our thoughts. Thus, we must think carefully of the bigger picture and any possible hidden options, before we come to a decision to act. With a complete picture from above to alter our perspective and attitude, we can then see with 20/20 vision before we form an opinion, or solution. Only with clarity in our mind, should we make effects to the environments and people around us.

Aristotle's thoughts on Metaphysics

It is clear, then, that wisdom is knowledge having to do with certain principles and causes. But now, since it is this knowledge that we are seeking, we must consider the following point: of what kind of principles and of what kind of causes is wisdom the knowledge? (Aristotle, Metaphysics, 340BC)

Metaphysics involves intuitive knowledge of improvable starting-points (*concepts and truth*) and demonstrative knowledge of what follows from them. (*Aristotle, Metaphysics, 340BC*)

Demonstration is also something necessary, because a demonstration cannot go otherwise than it does, and the cause of this lies with the primary premises/principles. (*Aristotle, Metaphysics*)

The first philosophy (*Metaphysics*) is universal and is exclusively concerned with primary substance. And here we will have the science to study that which is just as that which is, both in its essence and in the properties which, just as a thing that is, it has. (*Aristotle, Metaphysics, 340BC*)

The entire preoccupation of the physicist is with things that contain within themselves a principle of movement and rest. And to seek for this is to seek for the second kind of principle that from which comes the beginning of the change. (*Aristotle, Metaphysics, 340BC*)

There must then be a principle of such a kind that its substance is activity.

... it is impossible that the primary existent, being eternal, should be destroyed.

... that among entities there must be some cause which moves and combines things.

... about its coming into being and its doings and about all its alterations we think that we have knowledge when we know the source of its movement.

(Aristotle, Metaphysics, 340BC)

David Hume On Causation / Necessary Connection

It must certainly be allowed, that nature has kept us at a great distance from all her secrets, and has afforded us only the knowledge of a few superficial qualities of objects; while she conceals from us those powers and principles on which the influence of those objects entirely depends. *(Hume, 1737)*

When we look about us towards external objects, and consider the operation of causes, we are never able, in a single instance, to discover any power or necessary connexion; any quality, which binds the effect to the cause, and renders the one an infallible consequence of the other. *(Hume, 1737)*

Experience only teaches us, how one event constantly follows another; without instructing us in the secret connexion, which binds them together, and renders them inseparable. *(Hume, 1737)*

We then call the one object, Cause; the other, Effect. We suppose that there is some connexion between them; some power in the one, by which it infallibly produces the other, and operates with the greatest certainty and strongest necessity. *(Hume, 1737)*

Immanuel Kant

Time was, when she (**Metaphysics**) was the queen of all the sciences; and, if we take the will for the deed, she certainly deserves, so far as regards the high importance of her object-matter, this title of honour. Now, it is the fashion of the time to heap contempt and scorn upon her; and the matron mourns, forlorn and forsaken, like Hecuba her empire gradually broke up, and intestine wars introduced the reign of anarchy; while the sceptics, like nomadic tribes, who hate a permanent habitation and settled mode of living, attacked from time to time those who had organized themselves into civil communities. But their number was, very happily, small. Thus they could not entirely put a stop to the exertions of those who persisted in raising new edifices, although on no settled or uniform plan. (Immanuel Kant, Critique of Pure Reason, 1781)

This can never become popular, and, indeed, have no occasion to be so; for fine-spun arguments in favour of useful truths make just as little impression on the public mind as the equally subtle objections brought against these truths. On the other hand, since both inevitably force themselves on every man who rises to the height of speculation, it becomes the manifest duty of the schools to enter upon a thorough investigation of the rights of speculative reason, and thus to prevent the scandal which metaphysical controversies are sure, sooner or later, to cause even to the masses.

(Immanuel Kant, Critique of Pure Reason, 1781)

We create our world and environments with the actions of our thoughts, just as our thoughts create our reality, thus in reality, life is the sum of our thoughts, yin or yang your personal perspective. The physical world is in our hands individually as we perceive and create it, both physically by effect and mentally by our choices. The physical illusion of our perceived real world, is created by the senses of our body, sight, sound touch. These are all just waves of light, and vibrations of sound, that have been deciphered and given form from our physical brain which is subject to damage and distortions.

The Secrets of the Universe

~ The sole purpose of life is to process Gods breath of energy as we experience coexistence in a physical environment, a lesson in humility and substance. The test of our grounded conscious presence is to start with nothing and return with respect and admiration for not only our life, but all life.

~ **The New Universe** ~

In the beginning there was a vast universe with abundant life. In this universe there was a galaxy with a Blue giant Star of great magnitude. Through its cycle of life it was a glorious sight. Then at its end in an epic explosion, it disappeared. The massive energy and vibrations ripped a hole in space and time, this exploding into a new dimension of our reality. The force of the explosion created another universe on the other side of the black hole, and was then thrown out in all directions. In this new universe there was a great expanding void, one with much clutter and debris. The Black hole that formed the rip had by then started balancing the flow of energy that it had expelled. Life must have balance in the exchange of energy, you cannot have a charge without a source, and every source of energy has to be supplied with its consumption requirements to exist.

This vibration of sound and light creating the cymatics of our Matter and planets, thus, the evolution of life had started, the first particles vibrating together creating a planet, and then others eventually combining in space through the universally designed mechanisms of basic planetary cymatics. This creating the galaxies, planets, and stars within the universe, our life evolved from forming particles and Matter, through the frequencies and energy of vibrational sounds. All life starts in the form of frequency and energy, then Gas, liquid, plasma, tissue, and finally solids. Even the formation of a seed starts within the water of a plants life after the absorption of gas and water ((CO_2) and (H_2O)). The mixture of time waves of energy forming Matter and creating life, thus reality as we know it, and perceive it, although reality is not what we see, but what we decipher from our senses.

(This is explained later in the principals of Quantum physics.)

This process formed a large spiral galaxy that eventual formed our planets and suns, all having gravity of some sort, and an electrochemical particle type attraction bonding them together. The never-ending cycle of energy was then complete, the suns and planets of the each galaxy constantly orbiting the abyssal trash compacters of life as it constantly recycles energy and time without fail, our two-way filter of Matter and energy, if you will. Within this new universe there were ever turbulent times as more galaxies, suns, and black holes formed and grew. Gravity formed around the planets while they were trying to find direction, and form their individual orbits. Several collisions and divisions occurred. These forming smaller moons, Asteroids, and comets during their cycle through time, then one day appeared a large comet consisting mostly of frozen water; it crashed into a planet and caused great damage, throwing massive pieces of the dirt into space that later formed a moon. The ice melted, and created a great sea, The Sea evaporated into the atmosphere, and a large patch of land was revealed. Pangaea was its name.

The atmosphere and conditions were pleasant for the evolution of chemical life that grew from the seeds of space. Yet, the planet's core was still hot and molten. As the magma crept up through the land creating rifts, the volcanic minerals forced their way up through the rocks blasting their way into the air. These rifts and hot spots formed the mountains and seas while the heat and steam dissipated. Rain fell as the water returned to the lands through the passing of time, and the magma's energy slowly forced the land apart and into several pieces, but not before some plants, and other small forms of life, grew through the process of evolution. Great beasts were born, and a lack of human anarchy let the plants grow large and the beasts roam free. This until yet another heavenly rock fell upon the planet; this one devastated almost all life, and left the planet a cold dark rock for many years.

Then finally, A light broke the clouds, and the sun started to warm the earth again. There were many small creatures that managed to ride out the storm in one fashion or another, and as life found a way to return to the planet again, a primitive man starting to emerge from the chaos. This primitive man evolved and discovered fire. A step toward the construction and destruction of his desires, he soon fashioned some tools of use to work with, and as he began to build a civilization he discovered that he needed some rules and morals to live by. This because the population was growing and egos were developing into a path of chaos and ownership, so the chief sat down in thought to ponder.

The causation of a need brought forth a wise man with a conscious knowledge and control of his thought and energy. As the chief conspired with this greater consciousness of the land, they had a grand idea of freedom and compassion for those in need. Soon souls and minds were freed to think for themselves, and then there a set of 10 laws to live by was handed down from above.

These were basic morals for human compassion, conduct, and life, and then life was peaceful for a while. But after some time, additional laws to serve man's purposes were added, and then the confusion began. For many years this worked well for the rulers of the people until, again one day a man came and said, enough slavery, we are all equal in the creator's eyes. Enough working in fear of pain for pittance and food, and the people again thought for themselves and they saw this was true. Then there was enlightenment, compassion and love for each other again as they fought their way to freedom. They found joy within the starting of new paths within their journey of life giving hope and a new perspective, equal rights with respect for our individual personal freedoms. This was good until greed and jealousy set in, and the morals of men fell once again due to poor perspectives, and the feelings of discontent felt within the tides of status, ownership, and equality. This caused great battles and claims of property. Lines were drawn in the sand, and the wars raged on to protect the ego and claims of the self-righteous kings and leaders. Many years and lives were lost, and then the people started changing the tactics of their plight, playing games of betrayal, and deceit amongst the people of countries and governments.

We all know the pawns are almost always played first in the struggles of power and status, and this leads to a quest for financial power and control of the resources needed to persuade others with. Money, money, money, everybody seems to have their price. But, at what cost to their soul and our society?

We as individuals have the right to believe whatever we want to. But to proceed forward, we must accept a common good, instead of our individual desires. Unity is simply a change of attitude and perspective. The understanding that we all come from one source, and have our own beliefs, but are going to the same place, and the fact that in reality, we are all working toward a common goal. By putting the goodwill of others first, we would cause a cascade of goodwill toward everyone. It's that simple to change the world, a different perspective and thus, a different attitude. Have a great day and enjoy your journey through life, but don't forget to help create it, before you stop to enjoy it.

Physics constitutes a logical system of thought which is in a state of evolution, whose basis (principles) cannot be distilled, as it were, from experience by an inductive method, but can only be arrived at by free invention. The justification (truth content) of the system rests in the verification of the derived propositions (a priori/logical truths) by sense experiences (a posteriori/empirical truths). Evolution is proceeding in the direction of increasing simplicity of the logical basis (principles)We must always be ready to change these notions - that is to say, the axiomatic basis of physics - in order to do justice to perceived facts in the most perfect way logically. (Albert Einstein, Physics and Reality, 1936)

~ Any intelligent fool can make things bigger, more complex, and more violent. It takes a touch of genius - and a lot of courage - to move in the opposite direction.' (Albert Einstein)

'Simplicity is the ultimate sophistication.' (Leonardo da Vinci)

~ We are all children admittedly or not. Our growth is in the acknowledgment of the universal energy and consciousness. To enjoy our path, is to enjoy the journey with a positive attitude, this is because the light of joy is not an issue to find, but a container that we drink from. When we can enjoy the journey within, the world becomes a brighter place. Those who live in the present must constantly plan for the future within their thoughts, why? Because when we dwell in the present, we forget our passion for a better future, and the lessons we have learned from the past.

"All we are is a result of what we have thought' ~ Buddha
Thus, we must create a better tomorrow before we sleep.

A lack of projection creates a circle in existence. To proceed in a progressive way, one must create the proper perspective, and then a better day by laying the foundation for it. Whether you enjoy the journey or not, it is what you make of it.

The journey to enlightenment once attained has endless levels, and they are continued through our cycle of life, into the next plane of our conscious existence. The path is an adventure through our mind, and individual environments. Yin or Yang, Good or evil, the morals of humanity remain the same. It is the individual that sways to one side or the other by their perspective. Thus, the route to enlightenment is found individually, within the map of our time during life. Always take advantage of new accurate knowledge, the information can only enlighten your journey. The joy and gratification of enhancing your knowledge, will light your path to the reality of the world. An Ignorant mind finds distortion among uneducated thoughts. The mind holds all the cards, don't play with a short shuffle. Endeavor to enlighten your intelligence, this ultimately filling your soul with the truth in all things.

~ **All things appear and disappear because of the concurrence of causes and conditions. Nothing ever exists entirely alone; everything is in relation to everything else. There are two mistakes one can make along the road to truth. Not going all the way, and not starting. ~Buddha~**

~ People deal too much with the negative, with what is wrong. Why not try and see positive things, to just touch those things and make them bloom? ~Thich Nhat Hanh~

Relative to humanity and society, the lights of our souls make up the stars of our individual beacons. Dim or bright, they are a reflection of our soul. Each light throughout the night is a possible friend or foe, our perspective and attitude may vary as the honesty of a situation is revealed. Yet, with understanding and compassion, negative issues can become a positive common cause for solution.
Enjoy the beauty and light of the stars. they are there to brighten our night, only the arrogant fight.

By being there for our friends we are having compassion for their position. This helps, but we must have compassion for their perspective as well. We can help them through their issues at hand, by thinking logically while they are in a state of illogical emotions. Only when a person is calm can they think clearly. But remember, never shine your light of knowledge and joy in their face, but point it in a direction for them to follow. Be a lighthouse, and not a spot light, there is a difference between preaching and teaching.
The value and importance in our thoughts of compassion toward others is priceless in our quest for peace. We all earn what we deserve in life as well as success. United we stand, and divided we fall. By judging others, we are refusing to look ourselves.

When looking at our self, we find understanding and compassion for our path and journey. The value of seeing our self for whom we are is clarity in reality. Nobody's perfect, understanding this gives us compassion for mistaken actions. When pointing fingers, don't forget to look in the mirror, having some compassion for everyone's perspective, enlightens the attitude of reception to find a mutual solution for the issues at hand. A beacon doesn't shine in the eyes of others but lights the way for them to see. Our fear is the illusion of lack of control, with intelligence and knowledge, the only thing we need to fear is our inhumanity.

Life is a ride through the physical dimension of our current time, the thing we all seem to forget is that it's not the route of our path, so much as the perspective of our journey. With a proper perspective, the road is as clear as our destination. The traffic of our life is caused by our negative emotions, and our denial of the truth. These are formed by uncontrolled Ego's, and self-righteous perspectives. Without strife, there is only love, compassion, and conscious awareness within the elements of our life. One breath circulates through the lungs of humanity, the purity of our air is relevant to the attitude we walk the path with. With thought we create consciousness, by acting without thinking we create a naive, unconscious, and uncompassionate society. Think Oneness

The sole purpose of life is to process Gods breath of energy as we experience a symbiotic, and coexistent physical environment. It is a lesson in humility, and substance. The test of our grounded conscious presence is to start with nothing, and return with respect and admiration, for not only our life, but all life. Experiencing love and light is relevant to its expression. The light of joy is found within for us to share with others. The knowledge of life is found in knowing our self, and those elements around us. When all of our elements are combined, we find Akasha. The unity of humanity is found in the space of our individual perspectives. With an unobstructed view from above, the truth is always revealed below. Teaching is the sharing of truth, and learning is the acceptance of what you've heard.

~ Only two things are constant in life, resistance and perseverance. We all exhibit and reflect both, when we can accept the enlightening truth of our energy and being, then we can find inspiration to make a positive difference not only to ourselves, but to others as well.

The Pessimistic attitude

~ Don't be pessimistic. An empty glass contains no substance at all. Thus, to have anything in the glass at all, it had to be added to the once empty glass at some point in time. Once filled the glass of life always has volume. What concerns me is what thoughts it's filled with. ~Bret Varcados 2010 ~

Our perspective and attitude forms the coffee cup of life we drink from, if we add love and compassion to the cup, it always sweetens the flavor of our coffee bringing us joy. Therefore, with the alchemy of a positive perspective you can change your cup of lead, into one of gold. And yes, sometimes it takes a little conscious effort. But, the beauty of a dream exists in reality, only when it is processed through a cause, and the completion of our task, is always felt as a gratifying joy within. This reflects to those around us as inspiration. Your beauty may inspire many people in many ways, but the most powerful reflection you have to others, is that of your happiness and joy for life. The heart is the conscious soul's container, our vessel of universal energy and its element of thoughts transformation. It also magnifies the energy that our thoughts require to transform into the world of our physical reflections. To find inner peace of mind, we must look through our ego and into our heart, the result will be a clear picture of what's important to your soul, and the world as a whole.

~ Prince or peasant, the value of a selfless action is cause enough to inspire greater thoughts of our personal existence. The value of our conscious spiritual knowledge is increased exponentially with the practice of compassion. This is also seen as a reflection of inspiration to others. The ripples of sanity find substance in the thoughts of the humble while working their way through the walls of the ignorant. Before a thought in the still of the mind, we are at peace with our self and the universe. A motion is the result of a thought, and movement is a series of actions from that cause, without thought and motion, we cannot proceed or exist in reality, therefore we must think before we act, sound familiar?

There is a rule that states an object in motion tends to stay in motion. The same is true in sharing love and light, a gesture of goodwill or kindness, often reflects to the next person in the chain of personal encounters. Smile as you pass people, say hello to your neighbor, do something nice for someone you don't know. The effect of positive energy can then be spread like a wildfire within dry leaves.

The world is what we make it, the definition of unity, is many working together. We all have a light to share, some dim, and some bright. The dim lights often hang out together in the dim light of illuminating truth. It is up to the bright lights to share their positive perspective and energy, this brightening the light and paths of those in the dark, and illuminating the proper path to their future.

Love is the only thing that doesn't pass away, we always seem to have a soft spot in our heart for those we love, or have loved. Hate and despair, will pass with resolution of the issue. The only thing eternal is our consciousness, and the love we fill it with. People react to things the way they have been taught to. This is a reflex action and we really can't blame them personally, for the social environment, only their lack of personal self-control, personal choices, and actions within our symbiotic social environment.

A paradox? No, we may have been taught to react a certain way by our culture or family, but the individual still has the capacity to make a choice to do the right thing or not in spite of the common belief they might be associated with. This is because ultimately we are each responsible for not changing the way we think when we figure out that it is faulted in the principals of morals, greed or stature. These are formed from our illusion, and wish to be accepted by others among our peers. This is also known as our option of freewill, if applied in the proper direction, it can be highly beneficial to everyone, not just yourself.

~ We all have been given a great honor; life is part of your destiny, the Journey of life itself is the act of a promise. The promise is to return to our creator with eternal respect and admiration for life.

Bathed in the light of truth and understanding, we find our way to the light of mutual joy. By seeing our reflection in others, we can find satisfaction and love for our existence. Occasionally one must face, and overcome their own fears in order to find the light of self-discovery. But in self-discovery, we find a refreshing energy of positive thoughts. Our thoughts are our energy, positive or negative it is reflected back to us in the form of karma, due to the quantum mechanics of energy and mechanical cycles of life. Energy is the substance of universal and physical actions, our perspectives will always dictate our path and direction, as well as the enjoyment, or discontent that we may feel along the way. The value of one is the first number toward infinity and the last number of our individuality. When another one is added, we must coexist; this is actually a blessing because personally, and I think I can speak for everyone else, would hate to be alone in the world.

The natural order of life is to create and coexist; Good and evil have perfect balance. It's an individual's thoughts and actions that write the new page in our heart and souls records, the demons in our head, are the hungers of our selfish greed. When we act selfishly, this forms a habit of thinking in our perspective, and unless our perspective is changed to a respectful and compassion thought process, we will find ourselves growing greedier, and never able to have enough in life, thus never content with what we have. When one is content with themselves, they don't need shiny trinkets to prove their worth in society. They find that they are valued for their thoughts and not their stocks.

Joy and beauty are free in our world, the only price we pay for respect, is compassion, it's all a matter of perspective. A true friend accepts constructive criticism as advice, and not as an attack on their person. Sometimes emotions flare and this is forgotten, but a true friend will realize their mistake, and apologize for their arrogance without persuasion, but through our clear communication.

Teaching is simply the sharing of thoughts and knowledge, and learning the acceptance of information. We are all students in life choosing our own teachers. The lessons we learn in life, are the reflections of our choices. Today and tomorrow, will be created in reflection of your thoughts, may they be wonderful throughout your journey. If you're having a difficult day, you should seek out friends for support, if they don't have the time to listen, then you have to ask if they are really your friends. The issue of privacy is our personal perspective or feelings to conceal ourselves from others in society. If you have nothing to conceal, you should have no issues with others. Yet, due to our personal feelings of pride, we often make personal claim to an area. The feeling and need for privacy we feel, comes from our personal insecurities and doubts of social acceptance. This is due to the illusion of indifference.

The chaos of life is due to the duality and indifference found in the motives and thoughts of our personal perspectives on the major side, and the slight universal abnormalities found within time on the lighter side. Thoughts on theft, only a greedy self-centered, or desperate person takes others personal property, and those are the feelings we are trying to get past right? So, just respect others and don't it, good people would rather help, then have a person feel like they need to steal to survive. As we live, we create our own heaven or hell, when we have compassion, and joy in our thoughts; we create our own heaven during our physical existence.

When one sins upon the morals of society or themselves, discontentment and despair are created from the negative energies reflections, not only for the offended person, but also through karma and the law of returns, is eventually returned to the offender, this creating their own hell in reality. The journeys effective change positive or negative, is your choice. It always has been, and always will be. The value of our Compassion is the ultimate compass of our worth. We as humans in nature seek to find knowledge, the knowledge we seek in life is relevant to the experiences we encounter within our life. Along with seeking our purpose of existence, we quest for accomplishments in our life.

The real task in life is to improve our mind, and the perspective that forms our individual attitude. Logically, those in poor situations are going to have resistance getting there because, they are struggling already. To encourage the speed and evolution of our conscious change, we should eliminate the resistance of the other parts within our being by removing some of the negativity in the world, this letting us face the realistic problems of our consciousness, rather than the materials needed for our survival. The need for individual survival is relevant to the compassion of the others in the environment, as well as the social surroundings that we all coexist within. To leave a friend without a jacket in the cold should make you feel bad, leaving others without food, should feel the same way. Even if you can't see them, it doesn't change the fact that they are there and you know it.

It's funny, the people who have been poor, can understand the reality of life in a way fortunate people can only imagine relating to. Materialistic stuff is only baggage, our thoughts of love and compassion, are the only things we carry without physical effort, actually benefiting us in our realities. Therefore, they are the only things of real value. The beauty and joy of life are found within the light of our compassion. We must notice and draw upon them in order to enjoy and share them. They are the most energetic and inspiring perspectives we can have, in the absence of light there is only the darkness, and the poor attitude found in the despair of discontent feelings. When an issue arises, one should view the situation from a position of noninvolvement, in order to find the non-bias answers needed for the solution. This is because when we remove our emotions from the cause of issue, then we can easily find the answers needed to solve the problem. We cannot blame government alone for the problems of our current society, we are each responsible for our own environment, this includes the creation of causes and effects.

If we want change in our realistic world, then we must start by changing the way we think individually. Attitudes and perspectives are contagious whether we share them or not. As with everything in life, to proceed to a destination in any direction, you must first start from where you are, and then you can choose to proceed in the direction of travel, at a speed relevant to the force of your efforts toward the destination of your journey. But don't forget to apply more thought and action to accelerate along your path, or you will be left sitting in neutral in the traffic lanes of life.

Life isn't a mystery. God is the conductor of energy and thought in the symphony of life. Nobody makes the choices causing the effects on humanity, except for the individuals that exist within its society. Our thoughts and choices are grown from the seeds of our emotions. These are planted from within our interactions with others. With infinite individual perspectives, the only way to find balance in our existence is by using truthful communication and keeping compassion for each other in mind. Share the beauty and joy with others, and they will share with you. People take action and cause the effects on others because, Yin or Yang, they wish to gain something for themselves, materially or emotionally. If people thought about others as part of themselves, then we wouldn't be living in the world of greed and poverty that we currently do.

The world's environments and attitudes are created by the thoughts and desires of humanity as a whole. Majority rules in forming social attitude, just as it does in deciding the actions and motivations of a society. However, it only takes one person to make a difference to someone else. Emotions are the blessing and curse of humanity; they are the seeds of good and evil. The joyful balance of life is found between our Ego and Compassion. Being the victim of our own stupidity is our own fault because it is only due to the circumstances, and greed, of our preference without consideration of the effect. We are who we are, no less, or greater, than the next person. Ego is not something we can let go of, it's part of whom we are. Yet, we can acknowledge this and the prior statement, and then control our attitude and perspective, through our Ego. Otherwise we let our uncontrolled Ego, control our attitude, and the perspective we live with. The acknowledgment of the truth in our infinite conscious existence is all that is really required to give us a realistic perspective, and this putting our ego in check. We are all on this starship Earth, heading to the same place. It's time we realized this and make the journey enjoyable for everyone. We can do this by enjoying the beauty in life around us, while showing respect, love, and compassion, in our thoughts and actions towards others.

Our Ego does no good to us, or anyone else, unless others appreciate it. Two or more may disagree on a subject in reality, but it is always more important to proceed in a beneficial direction, then it is for someone to be right. Life is coexistence with others. Thus, the concurrence in cause and effect is required for us to move forward in progress. The attitude we carry with us through the journey defines our enjoyment of the path. To look past one's own perspective seeing and accepting the perspective of everyone, is to see reality and the world for what it truly is. Understanding reality lies in all perspectives, the view of the many, becomes the reality of the one because our attitude is shown to the world on our sleeve, as the greeting card of our presence.

Storms come and go, a positive perspective and attitude are important for a joyful existence. Seek the knowledge of what's important to accomplish in your goals, and then properly act upon the realistic problems that you face along your journey. Life happens on the path between our choices. The journey can be easy or difficult depending on your attitude. The degree of understanding is directly relevant to your perspective of consciousness. Those with a small conscious awareness, only grasp a small understanding of life. If we can expand our conscious understanding of thought and energy, then we can expand our understanding of the purpose of life itself. Solidity is an illusion; life is what we create within our thoughts. One's perspective is the only thing that guides their task in the journey of life, the actions and efforts of our heart and soul are always the realistic reflections of our thoughts and words. If they are not of equal substance, more personal effort or honesty may be required to solve the issues at hand.

As a viewer from above with beauty, joy, and compassion as our goggles, we can see a clear picture from both sides of an issue, and then come to a meaningful conclusion to everyone. You are perfectly constructed just the way you are to fulfill your purpose, regardless of how others see or treat you. Find your task, enjoy your purpose in life, and the energy of love will find you, and flow through you. The journey through our physical world is defined by our perspective of it. This is within your control, life isn't a ride, it's a game, and it's your turn. Sometimes a little patience is a virtue in the process of reaching our goals. And a refreshing break to change the pace is great as long as we stay the course and direction after our intermission.

In times of sadness we should reflect on the things that make us smile for joyful support of our perspective. ~<3~

As a side Note:

~ I find it funny people don't acknowledge that plants do have a consciousness. The very act of a plant growing toward the light is the acknowledgment that the plant is consciously aware of where the light is coming from. From the flowering cycles of a plant we can conclude that they have a sense of time in relation to the sun and moon. We scientifically know this because we can control the process. We can also determine that a happy plant is a fruitful plant, from observations and its bounty.

Global Peace and Conscious Evolution

I believe global peace and evolution will require a shift in conscious awareness, because we must have a leader and there is always someone with a thirst for power. We must always remember that unchecked and uncontrolled power corrupts uncontrollably. Our leaders must be joyful and compassionate in their perspectives, decisions, and actions, as an example for society to follow. Our actions and thoughts are affected by their choices that affect the masses. All things appear and disappear due to causation. Evolution of our awareness is the next step in life; its progress is being seen in our current reality, ultimately the social understanding our of humanities true origin, Individual mental abilities, and purposes, are the next step in our humanity's evolutionary existence. Anyone who refuses to change will eventually get left behind in the ashes of the phoenix, as the old ways get forgotten in the fires of our conscious rebirth.

Life isn't about how much you can create for yourself, but how much of a difference you can make to others. This is because, that is what you will be remembered for, regardless of how much stuff you have. The roots of our life are anchored with respect for our family, culture, and beliefs. The winds of illuminating truth and knowledge, brings us wisdom in our reality. But, if we do not hear or see them, then we are left holding an empty cup of understanding. The joy of life is always found within the light of our love, and compassion for each other. When we have the patience to look into the silence of our inner thoughts, we find the illuminating information about our conscious awareness. Seek the light of your internal insight, to fight your feelings of doubt and despair. We all naturally know what's going on, don't let your fear of acceptance blind you to the changes that are occurring to everyone.

We have to admit this to acknowledge it globally. Peace and compassion are in, war and deception are out. Greed and self-righteousness lead to strife, and discontent feelings of our physical individualities. This in an illusion of an individualistic world, the world is only the sum of its parts. The same goes for people, the galaxy, the universe, and God. Ultimately we are all part of him and he flows through us. People tend to like to agree because the Id, and Ego, seeks similar thoughts. Fortunately for all of us, the universal learned experiences of our super egos are starting to come around to the sanity of peace, love, and unity within life. But we must not give up the fight if we want things to change in our current social paths. We need to change our selves and the way we think individually first.

Change only happens, when an action is taken to cause an effect. The world only reacts to our actions. A thought is wonderful and has a lot of potential energy. But it has little effect in our immediate reality without the substance of effort. To have peace and unity, we must be at peace with unity. The path of your life is only paved with your efforts, and actions. If we only tread water, eventually we tire, and sink into hopeless despair. Choose to be proactive and swim for the shore.

The state of oligarchy we are finding our self in is due to a thirst for power from the rich, and a lack of effort, or proper knowledge from the less fortunate. This is most likely due to oppression, depression, or the stress from just trying to get by. If we do not participate in making the decisions of society, state, and country, then we are left standing in the wake of those who have nothing better to do, or those who wish make money from the process. Odds are that they may not have our best interest in mind. Most likely one of how much money they can make from us.

Choose to make a difference in your future and ours. Act when you see something wrong by drawing attention to it. The price of negativity, greed, and selfishness, is exclusion and pity from society. The value of positive thinking, effort, and persistence, is priceless throughout your entire journey. We always reap what we sow; time is only the pause between cause and effect. If a person only takes from a relationship, only concerned with their happiness, then they are self-centered in consciousness and thought. If one is self-centered in their consciousness and thought, then they cannot think of others, until they realize that they are actually part of the whole.

The Idea of Yin and Yang having balance is indeed true, it is our perspective and choices that lean to the positive or negative side of our quantum existence. The ego and emotions coupled with individual belief and self-perspective add up to the sum of our conscious thought and idealistic opinions. When we can focus on the beauty of the moment, and the effect of our cause, then we can make the decisions that lead to a beneficial, symbiotic, and coexistent existence. Our individual physical paths have been intertwined throughout history, thus the writings and records of our society's actions as taught in grade school (World History).

To deny that we are symbiotic and coexistent beings is insanity, the knowledge has been taught to us since our birth. God is the energy of life, which is equivalent to love in its purest form, all we are expected to do in this life is to learn respect and reaction, the choice of your path is easy. Love or hate; compassion and peace, or strife and violence, the sum of your perspective and belief, equals your attitude and morality for this cycle of your souls existence. GOOD or EVIL? More like joy or despair, your choice, always has been.

The happiest moments in life, are often found in the most unexpected places. The path of our journey is always filled with inspiration and beauty, if you take the time to see it. Only when the mind is calm, can your thoughts' find substance in the beauty that surrounds us every day. A conscious mind notices everything in its environment and then adjusts its main attention to the area's that need it most. Your life only consists of your past actions and the memories of what happened after you made the choice to act. The ride of our physical time on earth, is in reality, but a moment in the existence of our consciousness.

The experiences we gain in life are the memories we carry through our eternity. Your life consists of more than just today, and your time here. One should always think ahead to make progress in a preferably controlled direction. Fortunately we get to choose our memories in advance.

~ Life and Love 101 ~ A mandatory lesson in consciousness and coexistence.
**This time on Earth is worth 1,000,000 pts on your eternal grade.

Thoughts are easy to have, the process it takes to affect our reality is often more difficult. This is due to the complications caused by others, and our own procrastination. This is part of life, and they are the lessons we encounter from the choices we make. The spirit of your soul is shown in your attitude toward life.

The direction of your journey is always defined by the reflection of your personality. Thus, your attitude and perspective form your personality, and directs your path in life. Successful or not, life is always what you make of it. Your attitude is entirely your choice. Joyful, or Discontent, your choices have formed your environment, only you can choose to change your attitude and situation. Even the poorest person can find the treasure of love, and the joy of friendship with a positive perspective.

~ *The last of the human freedoms is to choose one's attitudes.*
- Victor Frank

The true value of a friendship is always relevant to its mutual respect, when one loses respect for another person or vice versa, the relationship suffers and usually pays with its social existence. Thus, a persons social worth and admiration are defined by their personal perspective, attitude, and projected respect for everyone else. The greatest challenge in life is the one we face several times a day. The one that many people often fail, it is the one that continually forces us to make decisions, yet it is really the easiest one to complete. The challenge you face daily is to be proactive in your future making your dreams come true. Take a chance, process the cause of your goals until they become the effects of your life. The freewill and determination we face the world with, is the only ammunition we have as we journey through life. A person armed with love, compassion, freewill, and determination, is prepared to conquer any obstacle.

If we don't choose to control the direction of our future, then we are then left following in the wake of those who do. Look inside and see who you really are. Accept it, and become whom you really want to be. The person we are is only cultivated by who we want to become. To find the Courage, Compassion and Connection of our Flaws, we only have to accept that we have them. The attitude we live with is based entirely on our perception of life, and how we perceive our future. The value of your journey is always determined by what you have done, and the amount of joy you have experienced while traveling through your individual path. Our Attitude is the projected perspective of how we perceive our current situation within our environment, relative to our life.

If you are content and happy with where you are, then your attitude is pleasant and joyfully positive, when you regret situations and are discontent with your decisions, or the situation within your environment, then you will obviously be unhappy, and have a poor attitude.

Learning to control your perspective and thoughts within the moment is learning to control your emotions and attitude in your life. This ultimately increasing your self-control during the chaotic situations that we all encounter throughout the day, if you are unhappy with your choices, you simply need to think smoothly and consider all the possible effects to your actions, before choosing to make them. This is commonly known as, making better choices.

Fortunately, within every choice there is at least one lesson, even if that lesson is simply **_NOT_** to do it again..=o)

Since individual perspective is constant and attitude is constantly felt and seen by others. Yet our attitude guides the balance of our personal perspective. Then to bring peace and understanding to the world, we must control our attitude and perspectives.

To do this we must look at our perspective of life, and the purpose for us existing within it. This is ultimately to make a difference to others, a Positive or negative one, is always your choice. But, Joy follows a positive effort, while negative effects eventually subtract from everyone.

~ Laughter cleanses the soul as rain cleans the air.
The sound of laughter calls to our friends and children.
The emotional effect of laughter lasts a life time.
The joy of laughter is always shared with those around us.
The energy projected from laughter can brighten a room and a day.
~ May your attitude in life bring you many years of beautiful joy and laughter. ~<3~<3~<3~ Bret Varcados ~2010

A seed is planted within us all, the water for its growth is found within a positive perspective. The earth of the soul is fertilized with the knowledge of Love, Admiration and Respect for all life, as with any garden the occasional weed or impure thought is sprouted from the unwanted seeds of chaos, these must be seen for what they are, a thistly weed that if left unchecked will grow into a thorny bush inviting self-harm and accidental bloodshed or regret. These must be plucked out of our mind before they distort our vision by creating a maze of confusion.

The cycle of growth is constant, and the winds of change often blow within our thoughts. Occasionally, we need a solid brace to stand straight toward the positive light and energy, our friends are there, yet our path is rooted by our family tree of belief. We are always free to grow and branch out within the journey as we naturally should when we form our own opinions, but by enjoying the journey within our perspectives, the path becomes a wonderful adventure in front of us, rather than a thorny maze of confusion.

The resulting effect is the easing of tensions before they form, and the ability to venture forward without fear of failure. Only after the cleansing and removal of old distorted ideas or cells can new thoughts and growth occur. Only when we have learned the lessons of greed, and self-righteous thoughts have been learned, will people turn back to what is omnipotent for the existence of life. As the Earth is cleansed of selfish greed, life will be renewed with new vision and insight. Only then will humanity remember humility, and an appreciation for the land, and waters of our creation. The children are our future on this planet. Always respect the land, and each other, and this respect will be reflected back to you and your environment.

~Intelligence expands with knowledge. Yet, knowledge has nothing to do with intelligence.

We must always realize who we really are, before we can create who we really want to be. A lesson repeats until learned, once learned, we naturally move onto the next one that is relative to our individual path. Reminders of the obvious are affirmations for the knowing, and lessons for those that need to catch up, and are willing to learn. ~<3~ Please excuse the mess during our construction. ~<3~

We, Is not a single person. We the people are responsible for the fate of the world. Not the president, not the military, but All of us. The governments are our tools to shape society. How many tools do you let run your day? Make use of them by taking action and making a difference, it all starts at home within your perspective, attitude, thoughts, and actions. The attitude of the world can only be the sum of its parts. The attitude of the majority always influences the opinions, actions, and perspectives of the individuals. Individually we are all responsible for the attitude of our environment. Thus, your perspective and attitude are directly relevant to the reality that we all live in. Do your part and share a smile, positive thought, or action with those around you.

The Balance of Life

Fear is found within the illusion of lack of control. We feel fear situations only because we don't think we can control the situation. To control our fear, we only need to think of the possible causes and effects before they occur, then proceed with confidence in yourself, to be able to react to them effectively. Life encompasses Yin/Yang, and Good and Evil. One cannot exist without the other; each keeps the other in-check while balancing the scales of life.

One gives substance to the other, while our choices lean one way or the other and time moves on in the common direction of evolution. Both of Yin and Yang, have a task in keeping us on track, the true path always lies in rising above the middle, when we step down to the negative side of life we are taking a step backwards on the stairway to heaven. Once the majority of us are at least one the same page with the same understanding, then we can raise the standard of the bar up to the next level. Humanity's perspective is currently one of making a judgment, which is better or worse. When we can see both sides without judging, but with acknowledgment, and compassionate thought, we can then see the bigger picture of reality within our environment, as well as those of the people we coexist with.

Then with a little logic, the solution appears as if it were always there. The type of path you follow is always defined by your perspective. What we must understand is that, Good and Evil exists in us all, the path of our proper conduct is found, by drawing from both to form a conclusion of proper morals and actions within a situation. Too much negative energy and you take away from the value of life. Too much positive energy and you become a facade of reality, self-righteous, and unbelievable. This in it-self tips the scales to the negative side of perspective and attitude, for those that haven't caught up to you. Only with the balance of truth and compassion can we find our self, and humanities salvation. To deny this would be lying to yourself and others. One's perspective is the only thing that guides their task in the journey of life. The actions and efforts of our heart and soul are the realistic reflections of our thoughts and words. If they are not of equal substance, then more personal effort or honesty may be required to solve the issues at hand.

In the sea of society and government the low tides of content, and the high tides of despair, form the riptides of our economic and religious indifference. When the perspective of equality and a proper attitude illuminates the shadows of our humanity, then the seas of society will be full of compassion, and then both society and humanity, will triumph in the war with itself. The joy of life is always found in our thoughts and their effects. Preferably these are pro-actively joyful and beneficial for all.

With the illusion of substance in our current and past reality, material substance has always taken for granted once acquired. In our new reality, our thoughts will have more value than our wallets.

The projection of a lack of respect, will earn a lack of compassion in a realistic world. To be respected yourself, you must first respect others. Mutual respect is mutual trust, anything less is a facade of character and fake admiration. Tension always builds before a release of energy, this is called the rebound effect, it happens in society, as well as in the planet. In the planet they are known as earthquakes. In society, it is known as discontentment, followed by anger. By thinking smoothly and enjoying the journey within, the path and task becomes an adventure and quest instead of a race and battle for material goods. The resulting effect is a controlled attitude, and resolutions to our arguments of discontent feelings that often inspire the violence in our society and personal environments. If our uncontrolled egos lose the logical thought process and a lack of emotional control occurs, this gives us motive for violent actions or other illogical actions.

Unless we are able to smoothly think through an issue, we often find that we have made a poor decision. Some of our thought-out choices wind up being lessons, so why self-complicate our life by jumping to conclusions and reacting without thought. Every day when you wake up, you make a choice to be happy or sad. The course of your path may vary, but the choice is always yours within the options given. Be proactive in your positive perspective. Think of the beneficial possibilities of the right choice and its effect. We usually know the effect of the wrong choice, this is another undesired lesson. Only by thinking smoothly, and seeing the other persons perspective can we find the reason for people's reactions. With a little patience before our actions, we can find the clear picture of the cause, and the mutual attraction to an issue. Then we can choose a proper positive reaction, with confidence in our and their personal satisfaction. With the right choices we always find joy and self-satisfaction in the completion of a lesson, this is due to the confirmations of our pre-thought actions.

~ Death is to life, as weekend is to a week. The conscious changes we experience during our time of life are the lessons we learn within the path of our journey. Thus, the attitude we learn them with, dictates the joy or pain that we experience within our life.

~ Any intelligent fool can make things bigger, more complex, and more violent. It takes a touch of genius - and a lot of courage - to move in the opposite direction.' (Albert Einstein)

~ Simplicity is the ultimate sophistication.' ~ Leonardo da Vinci

~<3~ In the absence of presence, love is relevant to the Bond and prior communications of its expression. Love is only lost when it is forgotten, the heart always remains full when it has been filled with admiration. ~Bret Varcados 2010~

The issues of the new era are not going to money but self and social awareness, in an archaic world, the journey within is omnipotent to the sanity of your soul's existence within society. The beauty of a dream exists in reality, only when it is processed through a cause. Thus, the completion of our task is felt as a gratifying joy within, and this reflects to those around us as inspiration. Your beauty inspires many people in many ways, but the most powerful reflection you have to others, is that of your happiness and joy for life. The world has been changing, because people find satisfaction in being greedy, and they are self-absorbed. Everyone finds the light of joy within a positive perspective, as do I. Yet, the battle of our choice and reason is always raging within our thoughts.

When the mind is raging and ideas have no focus, we must find our peace of mind before we can sift through the rubbish, take a break and some time, with some calm thought from our mind's eye, we can always swing open the door of understanding, and enjoy some light, along with a fresh breeze of stress free inner perspective before confronting a decision of major importance. In this way we can remove ourselves emotionally and find knowledge in the substance of the situation, and pluck out the issues in the order of importance. Because our inspiration to journey down the path flows through the attitude we carry though time. We must always find ways to view a better day during the storms of our time in our life.

The feelings we have for our neighbors are the reflections of their perspectives and actions, and the life we live, is based in our perception of it, and our picture of how it should be. The picture we draw is constantly being updated, it is only seen from within our thoughts, but it is shared by our physically by our attitude, and verbally with those we communicate with. The benefit to a positive perspective and attitude is most effective when the entire field shows support for the game of life.   But really, As long as the team works together, it only takes one Star player to win the game, and inspire future play. The boundaries of the field are only mental.
 ~ The only foul ball is the one thrown in discontent for the rules of our human morality.

I find it funny that some people go to church on Sunday, but they don't live the life of their faith. Their religion seems too only apply when they need it, or want it too, and then it is forgotten in the times of greed and argument. These are the times that religions and faith are written for and needed the most. If you buy a refrigerator to keep your food fresh, wouldn't you want to use it to keep things from spoiling? People have gotten spoiled due to a lack of practicing their faith in their actions. The value of your faith is relative to how much you live and share it on your journey.

The Book of any religion teaches that living with a positive energy, and a love for life within the balance of humanities morals, is a beneficial and joyful journey through life. God by any name is the being of conscious energy within the process of creation. He or she is the power behind the universal energy, and the gears of evolution. Even in quantum physics there is chaos in the observations of photons. Everything happens for a reason, out of causation. The reason why is not really our problem, unless it is a lesson. It is Gods knowledge and our hurdle, or gift to deal with. Our quest and task is to experience love, and share the light of our discovery for others to enjoy, benefit from, and share with others that they encounter.

Preaching is for the self-righteous, a true beacon of inspiration not only has its own light, but also reflects the light of others by sharing their compassion and perspective, relative to their perception of the issue, hopefully with a clear and non-bias, picture of the subject and issue.

When two people are in communication their paths and journeys are interconnected in temporary thought, and principal. The most difficult time to mind the rudder is during the storms of life. It is then that we must firmly grip the tiller, and smoothly plan our course to avoid the reefs. This is more easily said than done when emotions interfere with logic. So, take a breath and a moment to calm down, and then chose your path. The journey to enlightenment once attained has endless levels.

The knowledge gained is carried through to the next plane of existence, and the individual journey is an adventure through our mind and environment. It is a balancing of our conscious thought, spiritual life force, and Chi. We all do it subconsciously at different levels of spiritual acknowledgment. Meditation, yoga, breathing techniques, prayer, these are all forms of centering our self, and concentrating the energy of our thought.

Our path is found individually within the map of time. Within our physical time on earth, the friendships we make are priceless in keeping a positive attitude. They become the gems and treasures that we find on the path of life, and they are always added to our chalice during the quest to find love and acceptance. True friendships are based on Admiration, Truth, and Trust, joy follows when these are mutual. Distorted perceptions cause distortion in our perspectives when left unspoken about.

The beer goggles of belief often require cleaning to see the truth because, within the mind dwells three consciousnesses, the primal desire or Id, our intelligent thought or our Ego, and the greater consciousness or the learned experiences of our Super Ego. The ego is the battle field of our perception. When one has the perspective of self-righteousness, they are vain in their perception of life. Unity and peace are only obtained when the perspectives of all are considered. The destination to enlightenment has many paths, but the only one of importance is your own. Use this data at hand to upgrade your memory and CPU to include the options available to everyone within the path.

The quest for a peaceful life and the effort of the individual is what's needed to obtain the goal of unity and coexistence. Change is constant even though unseen, this is called evolution. As a pet grows but gains little change daily in the eyes of its owner, so does humanity evolve in the eyes of society. The followed path or enforced training is left to the captain and the crew with the most determination.

A Positive Perspective and Attitude

I always try and see the silver lining in a lesson, even in the worst lessons we gain the knowledge not to do it again. We can also learn from the mistakes of others, as these may carry a heavy lesson in our hearts. Life is how we perceive it. Our perspective and attitude of the moments, form habits within the neurons of our brains, a happy person habitually thinks happy thoughts, a sad person habitually thinks of negative thoughts. The benefit of a positive perspective is felt by ourselves, and seen by others as a beneficial conscious lessons. This is the result of a positive action, and the processing of a thought. An internal modification to our thought process and perspective before an action is all that is required to solve the issue of depression, and negativity. When sad we must think of happy times and focus on them until the feelings become a habit that helps carry us through the day.

There is no right or wrong path; there is only your path. The value of your journey is weighed by the effect on the environment, and others you coexist with. The purpose of life is to find knowledge, Love, and Joy, the task in life is to share that knowledge and love with others you encounter so they may enjoy life as well.

The adventures we choose in life provide the lessons, and knowledge that we gain within our journey. The more aggressive or emotional the experience, the deeper the knowledge is imprinted.

The admiration and enthusiasm for the passions we find in life turn into the little joys we seek throughout our day.

The school of hard knocks teaches us determination and compassion for others, through understanding by personal experience. The quest for love teaches us to never judge a book by its cover, and that patience is a virtue. However, a life without substance or direction; is like a car in neutral, you only burn fuel. When we give to others, it fills our soul with gratification. The gift can be as simple as a smile, or hug, the effects of your life that are left behind on others while you journey, will always show the size and volume, of the footprints you leave behind, as well as being what you will always be remembered for. Joy and happiness emanate from joyful people, if you're having a bad day, find someone who isn't and hang out with them for a while.

Note:
DON"T complain about your day to your friends. Instead, enjoy their company and perspective.

The intelligence we gain within the journey allows us to find ourselves, and experience other perspectives. This allows us to think smoothly and balance the load of life's baggage, effectively changing the way we perceive situations and make choices. Through our perceptions we can adjust our attitude, by realizing that negativity begets negativity, yet a positive attitude can change the status quo.

We can ultimately change our perspective to one of compassion and peace, by simply acknowledging and respecting the other person, and their perspectives. The path before you should be enjoyed while you're on it, only your attitude prevents this. When you have finished this journey and begin another, you can look back on the times you enjoyed, and use them as a compass for your future adventures and quests for good times. Always make the most of now. This way when you look back, you have a wonderful picture of your journey to draw energy form.

The value of your goal is often defined by the effort it takes to obtain. Freewill and determination are omnipotent in the quest after you discover your task. When you do, pursue it with everything you have. The light of joy is the reflection of your perspective. Smooth thinking during the storms of life empowers the ego to define the issues at hand. We do this by looking at them through a mirror of understanding found within our compassionate heart and soul. The brightest lights are always magnified by their reflection, to be a proper beacon for others; you must lite and reflect the compassion of love, and understanding. Within the crossing of our paths, we find the reflection of each other's journeys. Only when our hearts are truthful can we find meaning, and value within our emotions, due to compassion in our thoughts.

During this crossing of paths, we find people of interest to our mind and chemistry, each person we meet carries a fork in the road of life with them. The path we choose to take will often affect the journey, and possibly the priority of our goals. Therefore, all encounters should be thought of as an opportunity to change direction, or continue on as the rudder and beacon for our friends, during their storms of chaos found in life. A joyful, compassionate, positive perspective and attitude always seems to encourage our positive thoughts and actions in a progressively beneficial direction.

It is often said that when one door closes, another door opens. When the heart is saddened by mistreatment, it leaves room to be filled with more than before. Although an infinite container, the heart can sometimes get familiar with a negative source of energy, or a pure source can turn negative while in a relationship with lack of care and communication. This causes a paradox in feelings, and a wish to repair a situation that may not be in the best interest of either party.

Love and happiness are parallel lanes in life, yet love itself is a 2-way street. There must be reception for a true reflection and magnification of the mental and physical bond. Often if respect and admiration is only shown from one side, the relationship tends to vanish, and a lack of trust, is often the first sign of trouble.
The quest for happiness and joy must start with a love for yourself, and then this will reflect to others in your quest for true love and companionship. The Yin/Yang we find in life and thought will never change. The bigger picture is weighed within the balance of our personal morals. The ONE conclusion is to find equal value in everyone's perspective, this giving our personal perspective a broader view in reality.

The journey of a joyful path can only be found within our self. Our attitude controls our perspective. Spread joy through the world and yourself by causing ripples of light, within the stormy nights of those you encounter. This is all we can do, as we can only brighten the path of others. We are not given ropes and prods to herd with, and even if we were, 'You can only lead a horse to water, you can't make them drink'. If they don't know how, we can always teach them, but the choice is always theirs to make.

The ignorant are always arrogant in their convictions, a lack of knowledge, and refusal to see another perspective, causes blindness in consciousness. Love is the conscious light projected from our soul. Physical light is merely waves of frequency and magnitude passing through the eye, not even in proper form until processed in our mind. Love on the other hand, is felt in the mind and heart without having to be deciphered by the brain.

Therefore, it is not an illusion, thus logically, love and compassion are the only true energies behind life, and they are the door to endless joy, and enlightenment of the soul. Knowledge is the key to the door; seek to learn as proof for yourself. Then endeavor to journey through to the next level of play.

~ There will always be some daring singularity, and difference of opinion, but with mutual respect and compassion we can find resolution to our issues peacefully. ~ In Lak'ech ~<3~<3~<3~ Love, It's a good thing.. =o)

We all have a great vision of a better world and existence, the effect is only seen when we all create it. If you wait for someone else to begin the process, then you have already given up on the cause. We must create our own happiness and joy, before we can change the perspectives of others, this ultimately brightening the path for us all. Within the boundaries of our imagination, we find the inspiration and ideas for a better tomorrow. If we act today with these in hand, then we can effectively change our future, and then a better tomorrow becomes a reality, rather than just a good idea.

The wonderful thing about Karma is that we all get what we deserve in the end. The poor treatment of others tends to leave heavy gouges in more than just the emotions of both parties, but in the emotions, and memories of everyone in the environment as well. The social reaction then becomes the reflection of the offender's attitude. This is often multiplied relative to the quantity of others involved, and then this is systematical dealt to the offender, as spit balls of negative energy toward their personal ego and goals. This is because the law of karmic return is always compounded in its value, relevant to the thoughts and emotions felt by those who felt involved. Karma is really the simple quantum mechanics and cycles of energy.

Have you ever blamed someone else for something you did? Well, guess what, you all did everything, the economy is your fault, your life is your fault, and you're all to blame for every body's problems in life, some more than others, and that's no lie.

Let's get over it, and get on with life, we are all part of God and his consciousness, thus we are all gods and goddesses of our own environments, and our angels are the friends that surround us. Angels are everywhere, when we value our life we value what has been given us by the greater consciousness that was given us to cherish and learn from. When we attack each other verbally or physically, we are actually attacking ourselves and our environment from within. This is from our own feelings of discontentment, reflecting in anger, and then shown through our actions to others. To improve our self we must accept what life is about, the experience of learning and the chance to enjoy the time we have, rather than waste time on being discontent in the situations that we have created for ourselves.

The current path or issue isn't always our fault directly, but the series of choices we have made leading up to the event has caused it in some way. The issue is now to deal with it, and move onto the next task. There is no need to drag a lesson out if it has been learned. Sometimes those around us do ignorant and selfish things that affect everyone. Those are the people that need to be focused on. Arrogance of others personal space and perspective, is showing a lack of respect for their existence. When a person loses respect for the existence of others, the effect is felt on society as a whole, because the buck never stops there in habit, and the effect of disrespect is as contagious as the effect of compassion, Yin or Yang we all encourage the attitude of society.

The only reason for this lack of respect is personal greed or satisfaction. When the efforts of an individual cease to be effective, or they run into obstacles that they cannot conquer alone for one reason or another, it's time to lend a hand. Sometimes the opportunity never presents itself in the right combination of events for a person to advance on their own. This can be very humbling in life as time passes on. This is when people need the most help. Helping others is called being humane, and this is what life is about for us humans.

The humbled are all around us, most of them have never had, or no longer poses a physical address due to the duality in life, society's indifference, chaotic natural forces, financial tragedy, or even negative social energies, sometimes all of them. Much love and hope goes out to them all although, sadly sometimes by some, this is only given in the quest for personal redemption, for some guilt felt for possessing excessive material goods, personal issues, or other personal fouls against the morals of man, everyone seeks some kind of atonement or balance in life, instead of the honest love for equality and unity within life, that it should be in reflection of. However it is appreciated whatever the reason, we all have our individual perspective demons to face, and overcome in life.

To merely delay or put off a lesson by making small payments only compounds the interest within the lesson of life, and then as in finances, you will have paid far more for the lesson then you had to originally. The lessons in life are relatively free to learn, the only cost is our time and understanding. The heart has no pockets, and our ego is the only thing that holds us back. Of course our ego is part of our freewill and determination, when used properly it can have miraculous effects on society. However, when used poorly, it can ruin your reputation, and lives.

There are three voices of reason within the normal mind. These are the perspectives of our desire, logic, and moral conscience, or socially learned conduct. The voices within are commonly known as: The Id, your primal desire, the Ego, your personal and consciousness perspective of the situation, this is also our conscious point of decision to act within your realistic environment, and the Super Ego, the socially taught perspective, or the collective consciousness's perspective of the situation. Thus, someone that has little value for their Super Ego, would be ignorant and arrogant in their perspective, and someone unconcerned with their Id, would be thinking of others before themselves. And finally someone without an Ego, would actually not have much freewill or determination for advancing themselves. The battle of good and evil is a battle fought within our self as we react to the situations we encounter.

~ Sometimes in life we find ourselves treading water with the shore in site, due to the chaotic issues and indecision from others in our environments. We all must find our own path in life, if someone else can't find their bearings, you must take point, and show them the way to their salvation before it's too late for you both. There be sharks in them waters, nobody wants to get eaten. Live long and prosper,
~ In Lak'ech Ala K'in ~<3~<3~<3~

Sexual Orientations and Preferences, The effect of genes on sexual preference

Our Genes influence our thoughts through our biological construction; they are inherited from our parents, and their parents, they are strained through the birthing process, giving us our dealt hand of cards. The Epigenetics, or (over genetics) of our hand dealt in the early days of fetus development, turns the Genes on and off while battling the mother's immune system. The different tetragon's and other substances of her immune system attack our blastocyst at embryonic stages of the fetus, this forcing our new bodies to defend ourselves chemically. There is a biological war going on within the mother's womb until our matured fetal stage. This causes our DNA to form the XX or XY chromosomes and their variances. This process is what develops, and forms the variable chemicals and quantities within our individual containers, or bodies.

Genes influence our physical body and structure as well as the brain by constructing our DNA from the effects of our mother's body and environment, after birth, our evolution is relevant to our new environment, and is continuously affected by it, throughout our lives. A genes' purpose is to identify threats and new information, in an attempt to construct and counteract the destruction of our DNA. The relevance of this to our sexual identity is that the effects and circumstances of our conception, and the mother's environment, have direct effects on our physical form, and thoughts. Apparently to the point of common physical characteristics and ideas for perspectives, finger size has been known to be relevant to masculine or feminine attitudes.

The height difference of the index and forefinger being the point of interest, males have shorter forefingers, relative to the index or ring finger, assertive and competitive women have shown to have a shorter forefinger as well. However, this is more relevant to lesbians then to gay men. Using a PET and MRI, tests were done that displayed that the Amygdala was wired more for a fight or flight response in straight men and lesbians, while gay men and straight women, were wired more for emotions. They also found a more rightward asymmetry of brain use, in straight men and lesbians, this opposed to a more balanced use of the hemispheres in gay men, and straight women.

There are also theories of Gay genes being linked to chromosomes, the first called Xq28 by (Dean Hamer), and more recently there has been 3 others added to the list of suspects by (Risch et al), these are numbered (7,8,&10) But realistically, there are most certainly many different genes involved, to suggest only a few is almost comical in my opinion.

Chromosomes influence on biology and Desire

The Chromosomes purpose is to contain the genes and regulatory elements along with the nucleotide sequences within a DNA strand. It is an organized component of DNA and the proteins found within our cells, many of those cells make up the structure of our body, as we create more, we grow. I think it is a few years after puberty that we stop growing in size, because our cell growth has balanced with our cell deterioration, but that's just my theory.

Chromosomes are affected by the parents in the early stages of conception. Chromosomes are the essential unit for cellular division, they must replicate, divide, and be passed properly and successfully to their offspring cells to ensure the survival of their progeny. They can exist either duplicated, or unduplicated. Unduplicated they are a single linear strand, duplicated they form a crossing pattern, joined at the centromere. The Centromere, is the point at which the microtubules of a biological transferal attach to each individual strand, their general purpose is to reproduce. Females have 2 X's to form more estrogen, and a Uterus, and the male has one X chromosome with a Y, this creates more testosterones to form the Testes.

Which type of chromosomes disbursed during conception, is relevant to which one wins the race to the egg, and the circumstances the sperm encountered during the early stages of impregnation and pregnancy. There is only one sperm allowed per egg normally, due to an electrochemical barrier created by the copulation of sperm and egg.

~An interesting note: Women deactivate one of their chromosomes early on in development, which leads to the question of why, and what if they don't? And what happens if a male deactivates one of his by mistake or hormonal chemical imbalance? Could it have a relevance to males being gay? Just some thoughts to ponder.

Hormones Effect on the body and sexual preference.

Hormones affect the body because they are biological chemicals that are created by our body in response to our thoughts and senses. Our glands transfer messages from one cell to the next through our blood. In essence they are part of the body's communication system. Only a small amount is required to alter the metabolism of the cell and therefore the whole body.

In the cases of parental hormones having an effect on the fetus stages before birth, they would have to, but only from the point of conception from the father, from his donation, and then with the mother, not only genetically, but hematologically during her pregnancy. Prenatal hormones form at birth, from the mother and father as well as the medicines, drugs, plastics, and viruses that are encountered before the formation of the protective placenta. Even with the placentas advanced filtering system, the smaller tetragons, can be transferred through the filtering process, and all of these elements have an effect on the development of the blastocyst at the embryonic stages of the fetus's development. Through our biology we form our sexual identity, not from the sexual organs we are gifted with, but from the natural desires that are created from our mental and physical chemistry. There have been theories of antibodies in the mother attacking the bodies of the fetus, and this feminizing the younger male siblings in the family due to the mother building up antibodies from fighting the older brothers in the womb, and the mothers evolving immune system. During puberty our hormones force changes in our body to prepare us for procreation, and this causes us to think differently about whom we are, and what we desire in life in the long run. This is commonly known as the attaining of goals, and seeing the bigger picture, or growing up through maturity.

Hormones affect on our thoughts

The levels of Androgens in the body have a direct relevance to our sexual orientation. In lesbians as a group, there are slightly higher prenatal testosterone levels than in straight women, also apparent in some gay men, was the exposure to higher levels of fetal androgens. Since hormones are only passed through the blood, this brings us back to question of what women eat and do while pregnant, and what has been done by both parents, prior to the conception that may affect fetal identity and the physical body's structure during development.

Androgens are the hormone steroids that control male characteristics, but they are also the original steroid, and the precursors of estrogen, the female sex hormone. In the male its function contributes to Testes formation, prevention of female organs in males, sperm production, fat accumulation, muscle structure, aggression, and it has even been suggested that Androgen alone, can change the structure of the brain in several species, producing sex differences. Therefore you could say that a person's sexual preference, is derived from not only our parent's genes and chemical substance at time of conception, but it is also affected by the mothers emotions, while she is pregnant, and possibly the entire environmental attitude that she exists in during the early days of pregnancy, as well as our early childhood years of learning and development.

Personal Statement and Conclusion

Sexual Identity is formed at birth. A person does not turn gay because of society unless they have had an attraction to the same sex in the first place. They either have had questions of their sexuality since birth, or they knew they were gay from birth. People may wish to indulge in relations with the same sex, but this is due to natural hidden feelings they have had, or a lack respect, and admiration from the opposite sex within their environment.

Sometimes a curiosity, and possibly a preference may form from curiosity, but that would be a short lived experimentation, unless there was some confusion of sexual identity since birth. The effects of testosterone on the brain at birth determines sexual identity, this along with the aide of our luck of the draw during our conception. This may be relevant to our parent's genetics and emotional thoughts during pregnancy, followed by the environments and attitudes in our environment within the first few years of life.

Once puberty is reached, the libido along with our inherited and learned personality drives our individual sexual preference. People may also choose to act gay because of the events in their life, or the failed interactions with the opposite sex, but most are born with their preference encoded in there DNA and is not a choice, but a natural reaction of biology.

The debate of homosexuality really in my opinion is pointless and prejudice of difference. People are who they are, and can become whoever they wish to become. The choices we face every day force us to make decisions. These decisions are based on our personal belief, as well as popular opinion. The Ego and pride are our personal judges while our making decisions. If people would respect, and admire each other for whom they were as individuals, and not for their sexual preferences or characteristics, not only could our society get over personal differences, but the world could get on with making a better tomorrow for everyone.

Poor perspectives and attitudes are the problem with our society. Everyone thinks theirs is the only correct one. But, life is about coexistence, and this requires mutual respect and compassionate understanding from everyone at least. It would really be nice if we could admire each other for the being that they are as they are, but one step at a time. ~ In Lak'ech Ala K'in ~<3~<3~<3~

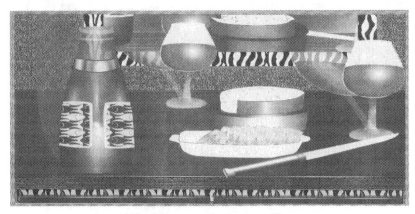

The Ego and Controlling it

Since the Id, and the Super Ego battle over primal good and evil, then the Ego is the referee, and judge in the debate. It is there to veto, or carry out the orders of our thoughts. What do you suppose the Ego, and Super Ego could do if they actually communicated, instead of directed each other? To find yourself, is to balance your life, with your knowledge and intelligence. The most influential consciousness we have is reflected through our Ego, the Superego is a collectively learned and voiced opinion of the greater consciousness. It tends to be the more intelligent perspective realistically, thus listened too usually as the authority in the discussion, when we go against it is when we usually get into trouble.

When one can effectively communicate with the Superego instead of just listening and reacting to it, then one can find awareness, and self-enlightenment. The battle always lies within, before we chose to act. To act without thinking smoothly, is throwing water on a grease fire. Our personal perspective of right and wrong is what we use as our personal compass of conduct. The north pole of our compass can always vary depending on the positive or negative influence of energy and choices within our environment. However, only when equality is found in the value of others thoughts, will equality and peace be fully attained on Earth.

The journey within our mind is self-grounding within our familiarity, and this focuses our personal thoughts and energies. When we do this, we can recharge our energy and understanding of life. This is omnipotent to practice for the sanity of the soul. It's called personal meditation, and it only takes a few moments a day, but the benefits last a life time. You brush your teeth daily to keep your mouth clean. You meditate daily to keep your mind and soul clean. This must be done before you can keep a mind and body clean of impurities realistically.

Age has no true wisdom other than having made more mistakes. A lesson always repeats until learned. Learning from our mistakes is the most important part of our path to continue on in a positive direction. To err is human; to correct our errors of the past is the task. The only thing standing in the way of cause and effect is the proper process.

In our silence we find the wisdom of peace, in time we find change, in change we find intelligence, with intelligence we find the truth, with the truth we find Knowledge, with Knowledge we find our consciousness, with our consciousness we find a possible future of death. In death, we find that we are an immortal ball of conscious light and energy, and a new journey begins. Thus, the cycle of life itself repeats. We have to take the good with the bad to see the clear picture of reality. But, this gives us our compass and bearing for future choices. The physical self is always an expression of our compassion. The effect on others Yin or Yang is caused by our emotions and perspective.

The beauty of coexistence is the time we spend with each other. When we as individuals realize that everything we do is a reaction to our feelings and perception, then we can acknowledge this, and logically think about our reaction before we act them out. If we perceive our self as individually the most important being in our life, then we are racist against humanity, and we become self-centered in our perspective and attitude. The acknowledgment of the fact that we are all born from the same cloth or compound of Matter should be the first clue to equality in life. The next is the fact that we all as humans have pretty much the same structure and shape. Although this is purely an illusion, as everything in our reality is actually a mirage made real by our senses and interpretations of energy and vibrational frequencies within our mind. The knowledge we are given can be flawed in principle, as it is an interpretation of a cause, effect, and reaction.

The only true facts, are those we learn for our self, or that have been proven to be true from our past lessons and experiments. The point is that as our ego interprets what is being seen and heard, and reacts to it. The Id wants to serve itself; it wants protection, satisfaction, or reproduction. This is derived from the Yin or Yang options introduced to our environment. The Super Ego wishes us to advance and take a chance by stepping forward into a new lesson, or warns us of possibly stupid mistakes, relative to the situations that arise in our environment.

This presents the battle of choice to the Ego, the beauty of this relationship is that it is our Ego that has the final say. Of course this is a curse as well because, sometimes after a while of success, the Ego can get over inflated, and then an individual can perceive themselves as more worthy than the next being. This is when it gets reflected back to those we coexist with as an attitude of egotistical narcissist. This reflects a negative attitude from those who know, and feel equal in value and presence.

Depending on personal intelligence and enlightenment, this could lead to strife if not mentally controlled and dealt with in a calm manner. Again, we have to take the good with the bad in order to see the clear picture of reality, but this gives us our compass and bearing for future choices. When we can step back and see all the sides of a situation, we can effectively find a solution and communicate our idea and perspective by debate. Even if we have the better idea, and the other perspective insists they are right, or vice versa.

Without the attitude of a hurt or a bruised Ego, followed by the common emotional outburst, and by thinking smoothly, a clear picture and perspective is found on the neutral ground of understanding, and then a resolution tends to appear and floats above the issue as a solution. Without a damaged or out of control ego problems are easily solved with honest communication. Simply put, when we can control our ego, we can control our attitude and vice versa. Whichever route is easiest to personally comprehend and follow for logical thinking should be sought. Take a walk by yourself, meditate, pray, listen to some relaxing music, sleep on it, even take a drive, A calm mind is an intelligent one.

It is time to let go of your preconceived ideas, they only set you up for disappointments, and the despair of discontentment. See every situation for what it is, preferably from the other person's perspective for a moment if you can, the result is a clear understanding, and honest resolution to the issue or argument. The conscious compassion that we show for our self and others is reflected in our attitude. It must be controlled to effectively make the proper decisions. To do this we must change our perspectives of life, we once thought the world was flat. Through adventure and knowledge we found the truth. When we think that we are alone in the universe, this is using the same logic that we used to determine that our world was the center of our galaxy, or that our sun is the center of the universe. Knowledge is freedom of conscious confinement.

A single person is no greater than the next in their physical form. If we deny change, then we deny ourselves the chance to appreciate and learn new things. Without advancement we are stuck in the past. Only when new adventures are taken may we enjoy the excitement of new territories. Venture to take a step forward in a positive direction, and enjoy the beauty and attitude this will create in the reflection of your freewill and determination.

We should all strive to befriend all life, some may be of opposite energy, and in this case we must try and reflect the light of attraction found within mutual understanding in hopes that it will refract in their energy as a positive influence. Only when a union of truth comes into balance are we truly friends and lucky to have touched another's heart.

Lebnis wrote; *'Reality cannot be found except in One single source, because of the interconnection of all things with one another'.*

United we stand for the good of humanity. Individual greed is the enemy, even when it is for self-preservation. We all profit as a group by working together, if we can value each other as equals on the team instead of having superior, or inferior personalities, and characteristics. Then we could settle all the issues on our plate with the ease of an agreement. The only thing our uncontrolled Ego gets us, is into trouble with our self, our loved ones, and society. Anger begets anger, love begets love, and compassion begets compassion. Life is a reflection of our Ego's attitude and perspective. When you open doors with a bad attitude, you find them closed to your perspective on the other side, and then your journey heading uphill.

There is a Solution

To achieve Unity, There are a few things we need to acknowledge:

1. No one is any better than anyone else. We are all made of the same substance, some maybe more mentally or physically challenged than others, but that only makes their journey more difficult. Let's not make their journey any more difficult by personal judgments, and opinionated actions.

2. Everyone has their own perspectives and beliefs. (*As individuals, it can be no other way*). The challenge society faces, is focussing on the common good with so many different perspectives.

3. All things are made from a common medium, thus are connected in the cycle of   Life.

4. People have the freewill to choose the path of their choice, from the options that   are provided from the effects of others choices and actions in the current environment.

IN WAR: RESOLUTION. - IN DEFEAT: DEFIANCE. - IN VICTORY: MAGNANIMITY. - IN PEACE: GOODWILL." -- WINSTON CHURCHILL

"And in the end it's not the years in your life that count. It's the life in your years." --Abraham Lincon

ALL THAT WE ARE IS THE RESULT OF WHAT WE HAVE THOUGHT. ~BUDDHA~

Reading, after a certain age, diverts the mind too much from its creative pursuits. Any man who reads too much and uses his own brain too little falls into lazy habits of thinking. ~Albert Einstein~

~ WE ARE BUT PENNY'S IN SOCIETIES POCKET, GAINING CHARACTER BY USE.. TO SHOW ONES TARNISH IS POINTLESS, WE ALL WEATHER THE SAME, SHOW YOUR VALUE, NOT YOUR WEAR. ~ BRET VARCADOS ~ 2010

~ When one is humble, he requires not riches, and physical items of value to be rich. He finds wealth in peace, and compassion. He finds joy in helping, and giving to others. He who is humble in thought and attitude, finds the treasures of life, within the substance of his actions ~Bret Varcados.~ 2010

~ The individual must not merely wait and criticize, he must defend the cause the best he can. The fate of the world will be such as the world deserves. ~Albert Einstein~

~ Happiness and joy are the result of positive thinking throughout the day. When you doubt yourself or your destination you cannot be happy or joyful. The discontent of not knowing fills the mind with doubt. ~Bret Varcados 2010~

Our conscious life in the form of energy never dies, it only transforms into different conscious levels of existence while we continue the cycle of life as the creator's children. We are constantly learning new lessons as time passes on, light is the effect of subatomic particles being accelerated during the creation of energy. Life is energy, within a defined structure of self-consciousness. It serves the purpose of providing movement, and conscious change within the universe. We are a symbiotic plasmatic being, coexisting with the planet and each other in a universal dimension that is one super macro cell with individual parts, within the body of God. The definition of life gives heed to an abundance of options from our perspective, intelligence, and belief. But the definition of time remains the same.

As per all the grand calendars, there is a cycle to life. Thus, within life itself, there is a cycle. You cannot remove parts from a whole, and call them independent, without causing the whole to cease to function. Those who do not understand, and disagree with science and logic, which are the basis of humanities' progress, are ignorant of the realistic problems in the universe. Thus, they are unconscious of other perspectives, and the reality of the truth. The truth of life is found in the knowledge of our thoughts, and energy. The energy of thought and the creation of fundamental particles are the essence of life itself. If we don't believe in science, then we are ignorant in our beliefs of reality. A fact, because science is proven facts, and not perspectives, we are all part of the whole, and the body tends to call for what it needs, when it needs it.

We often fear what we don't know, or are unfamiliar with. Fear, is also sometimes due to the distortion of truth, or a dilution of our perception. No one knows who someone is. They can only see their effects made on humanity. The greed of the golden egg has distorted the morals of society, this defeating our purpose in evolution toward a positive and beneficial advancement into the future. Without change, we can only move in a circle.

Those with little purpose and determination usually have a life empty of substance, and fulfillment. Progress requires freewill, determination, intelligence, and the imagination to find the solution to the problems at hand. Even if the effects turn out not to be what we wanted, there is always a lesson learned. The value of our effort is found in the cause, and the final result. If there is no change in thought, and we do not learn a lesson from our past mistakes, then there is only wasted time, and effort within our journey.

Some things in that we belief in and cannot be proven by science, this is called faith. We all have the faith that the world won't end tomorrow. This cannot be proven by any means other than determination. This could be affected by a chaotic catastrophe of some sort in reality, but what would really happen if everyone thought the world would end tomorrow? What do you think the effect would be? Thus, Faith rules our reality, because of our belief in it. The fight for progress in our reality requires idealism, and courage to combat the ignorance, and arrogance, of humanities own indifference, and personal Perspectives. Reality is proven facts, along with the ideas of imagination, and determination. These cause the effects of our actions.

When one becomes self-aware and conscious of not only themselves but others, one finds themselves at ends with humanity, but at one with nature. We must have faith in humanity and spread light to those we encounter. This bringing peace, and love to society, by shining light into all the corners of the world. In life, correlation becomes causation when it is apparent something is wrong and needs to change. The correlation between continents and countries, has determined that something is wrong with the way society has been treating humanity. This bringing the causation for change in our procedures and actions, it's time to wake up and smell the coffee, this pot has spoiled, and it's time for a fresh kettle. Anyone else awake yet? I'd hate to drink it myself.~<3~

We are all part of Gods subconscious. His dreams are the substance of our lives. It's time for some better dreams don't you think? Personally, I'm getting a little bored with the one that keeps repeating. In Life two things are constant, resistance and perseverance. Only with endurance, and compassion in our determination, can we make a difference to others, effectively changing our environment and other perspectives. Life is the challenge to advance in conscience before we return to sender. ~ Just a thought..=o)

We create our world with our thoughts. Each day presents a new page to write in our book of life. We can only truly love others, when we are peace with ourselves. Each path is unwritten until defined by our decisive actions. With silence and wisdom, we find the two-sided coin of compassion and joy. The gems of life are found along the path of our journey with in the friends that we encounter.

The journey of our life is a quest for mutual respect, and admiration. The balance of our Ego, Yin/Yang the cause for our actions dictates our perspective and polarity of our individual coins of life. Only with a clear picture of our self, can we see that heads up is always a preferable position to take in life. With a positive attitude and perspective we can chart new territories for the paths of our quest. Always try and have a blessed journey, and enjoy the beauty and attitude that you create in your path, as well as others.

There are a few truths that we have to accept while finding personal salvation and the enlightening path to our spiritual existence. Every part of the universe was created from an explosion in space. This explosion was actually, the implosion of a Blue Giant Star in another universe, or dimension. The cycle of life must exist in all things continuously. Thus, life is the evolution of a being, and every being has a sub- consciousness that desires to create ideas, and more life, this as well as, an active consciousness to control our decisions based on, and influenced by our emotions and beliefs, as it reminds us of our past learned experiences. And finally a unified consciousness that tries to balances the Yin and Yang of our morals. These are all facts and not opinions. They are commonly known as the Id, Ego, and Super Ego

– Love is the capacity to take care, to protect, to nourish. If you are not capable of generating that kind of energy toward yourself- if you are not capable of taking care of yourself, of nourishing yourself, of protecting yourself- it is very difficult to take care of another person. In the Buddhist teaching, it's clear that to love oneself is the foundation of the love of other people. Love is a practice. Love is truly a practice. –Thich Nhat Hanh–

Science shows us that we are made of energy. Our faith teaches us that life is meant to be good and fruitful in the quest of love and existence, that sharing with each other and making an effort to help others is beneficial to our personal journey. The transformation of negative energy into positive energy is the alchemy of life.

A peaceful, joyous, and gratifying life is always beneficial to all within our environment. Life really isn't a mystery. God is the conductor of energy and thought in the symphony of life. He is the breath of life, and we are the lungs of his body, nobody makes the choices causing the effects on humanity except for the individuals that exist within its society. Our thoughts and choices are grown from the seeds of our emotions, and these are planted from within our interactions with others.

With infinite individual perspectives, the only way to find balance in our existence is with truthful communication, and compassion in our thoughts for each other. Share the beauty and joy of life with others, and they will share with you. People take action and cause the effects on others because Yin or Yang, they wish to gain something for themselves. If people thought about others first, we wouldn't be living in the world of greed and poverty that we currently do. The world's environment and attitude is created by the thoughts and desires of humanity as a whole. Majority rules in forming social attitude, just as it does in deciding the actions and motivations of a society. But really it only takes one person to make a difference to someone else.

~ You are perfectly constructed just the way you are to fulfill your purpose, regardless of how others see or treat you. Find your task, enjoy your purpose, and the energy of love will find you and flow through you. The journey through our physical world is defined by your perspective of it. This is within your control, life isn't a ride, it's a game, and *it's your turn*.

~ In Lak'ech ~<3~<3~<3~

~ Humanity's salvation is found in these thoughts ~

1) Love is universal

2) We are all part of a single entity, with our own perspective and consciousness.

3) Spreading compassion creates, Love in our existence.

4) Being human, is a state of mind.

5) Within our past, are the lessons we need for a better future.

6) We must love ourselves, before we can love others

7) By sharing our thoughts and compassion, we can bring joy to the world.

8) By respecting others thoughts and perspectives, we can avoid violent

   confrontation.

9) Freewill and determination. Guide our journey, and pave our path.

10) All life occurs and operates in cycles of existence, and evolution.

11) God, Radiates through all things as the energy of life, and the conductor of our creation.

 12) Conclusions should always be based on proven facts. Scientific experimentation and confirmations, confirm that life originates from the fundamental particles of thoughts, forming the Matter of our substance from the cymatics of energy, frequency, vibrations, and time.

13) Our universe and existence. Is just part of a larger being, on an exponentially larger scale of life, we are literally part of a being called God.

Taking Charge of our Future Destination

For ages the predictions for this time in history have been known as a planetary alignment on a universal scale, and this is most likely to cause great changes in a lot of things, but all that the Ancient Mayan's, profits, scientists, etc.., are really saying or proposing is the end of a cycle, and the beginning of another after the event. We really don't know the effects of the process, but scientifically and realistically we can all see that something is happening to our planets' geological cycles, and weather patterns. We can also see the social state of our planet, appears to have begun radical changes itself, all this in a relatively short span of time considering the age and lifespan of our planet.

The frequency of events appears to be speeding up as we approach the epoch, and event horizon of the predictions and a conscious awakening seems to be occurring at an exponential rate. The black hole at the center of the universe has begun to radiate waves of subconscious energy, and the world is beginning to open her eyes for the first time to new perspectives. The journey on the horizon is unknown, yet predicted, and people are conscious of it. Yet some are still unaware, or in denial. Evolution happens in stages, if we miss the train, then we get left behind wondering what happened, as we discover that we weren't paying attention because of our ignorance, or arrogance. As the Phoenix of conscious awareness takes flight, the ashes of the arrogant and ignorant, get left behind in the dust. The impending galactic planetary alignment and our carpooling through the universal plane of existence, is created by the universes central Black hole, as part of the semi mechanical universe. Oddly enough, the cyclic passing of Niburu, also known as the destroyer, is supposed to be occurring at about the same time.

Correlation?. Maybe at least some causation for reconsidering our old ways of thinking and thought process, my thoughts then venture to, what will really happen?

~ Some predict a solar flare burning the earth to a crisp,

~ Some say earth's magnetic poles will shift, and the seas will overflow.

~ Some speak of the 10th planet Niburu. The Destroyer, Will come and cause havoc on our magnetic fields, causing devastation in its path, that's if we're lucky enough for it not to hit us. If it does, it's because we have trashed our planet, and someone pushed the reset button.

~ Some Say a New World Order will begin.

~ Some say Judgment day, and you had better ask God for forgiveness by May, 21st 2011. Because after that he is not taking any more applications and you will burn in the rivers of fire and despair after his final return.

A lot of predictions and conjecture but, realistically all we know is that there **_Will Be a_** change. ~ Yet, we control our own reality. Now, let's think about this for a second.

~<3~ All that we are, is the result of what we have thought. ~Buddha~
~<3~ He is able who thinks he is able. ~Buddha~

With all this mostly negative energy being thought of, What if someone suggested a positive change? Maybe something in the line of a DNA upgrade from cosmic energy shared between the planets, and passed through a thin conduit or plane of existence that focuses our spiritual energy, people coming together in thought and creating a positive change, something like that ~<3~.

With all this energy, that is ultimately going to be flowing through the universe, and us. If we could collectively think, and focus it on an enlightening outcome when the time draws near, then we could make a choice and possibly an effect. Because we create our own reality, we can all create a new beginning, instead of a faulty ending. Make no mistake. Anyone not prepared consciously for the possibilities, could possibly die of fright upon the precise night? Yea right, well maybe, you really never know when our time will come, could be tomorrow, but in any case.

The natural forces of the universe are beyond our current scope, and out of our control. So, if we can control our sails of fear, and our tiller of conscience, then we should be able to set our proper heading, regardless of what the event happens to be. The signs are all around us, all you have to do is look. With great change coming, I would think to stand together in positive unified thought, would be far better than huddling by ourselves in fear of the unknown. Our thoughts can create a great or poor day. The effect of love in a bright beam of light, might just light our way to salvation..~<3~

~ *We believe that an informed citizenry will act for life and not for death. ~Albert Einstein~*

~ The individual must not merely wait and criticize, he must defend the cause the best he can. The fate of the world will be such as the world deserves.~*Albert Einstein*~

~ **Chance favors the prepared mind,~ Louis Pasteur~**

~ So if we love someone, we should train in being able to listen. By listening with calm and understanding, we can ease the suffering of another person. ~Thich Nhat Hanh~

Nonjudgmentally, I have to say we all have the right to believe what we want. Life really isn't about what we believe, but how we carry ourselves while coexisting with others. Our perspective of life is the sum of our choices. When individually we all care about each other, our love and compassion are then reflected back, and received from the world around us. This helps form a positive attitude regardless of our situations. Shit happens, it's how we handle it as an individual that leads us to the way we handle it as a group. The sum of our conscious existence cannot be any greater than, the sum of our individual perspectives. When we are all on the same page consciously, then we will find Akasha and heaven on Earth, Teaching is the sharing of thoughts, and learning is the acceptance of the truth.

The Messiah's work is only to deliver a message and lead the way, I don't know where he is, but we need to make a move on our own. It's up to humanity to make our own decisions and act in accordance, as usual. The consequences of our choices have been known for a long time, time is drawing short and the Phoenix nears its destination, the choice is still yours for now. But evolution will change us in one way or another with time. We can either fight it, or go with it. Love or Hate, when humanity finds an absence of strife, then individually we will all become Akashic in consciousness. Gods Breath is the conduit of human energy.

Energy is God's love in motion; one breath circulates through the lungs of humanity. God's love energizes our creations, as we transform his energy and our thoughts, into the effects of our reality.

Our lights may dim in perspective of our belief, or attitude, but there is always joy to be found in life if we look for it. The beauty of our planet is there for all to see, and appreciate. The dim light of a poor perspective is further distorted by a poor attitude in life. We aren't candles, but flashlights with batteries powered by the effect of our love and compassion for others in our life. None of us would be here without the love of our parents and their part in the cycle. With an assured belief we find the knowledge of truth.

We are conscious beings of light trapped in our unconscious bodies of cymaticly bonded substances, an illusion of solidity, exchanging o2, for Co2 while doing our individual part transforming Gods breath of life and energy, into the motion of the universal body as the cycle of time continues to advance through infinity. With dreams of hope, the freewill of our imagination, and the determination of success, we live our lives. The path of our journey, swayed by the winds of our perspective, and the emotions of our confusion, the life we live is determined by the value of our love and compassion for others. When we act selfishly this forms a habit of thinking in our perspective, unless our perspective is changed to a respectful and compassion thought process, we will find ourselves growing greedier, and never able to have enough in life, thus never content with what we have.

When one is content with themselves, they don't need shiny trinkets to prove their worth in society. They find that they are valued for their thoughts and not their stocks. Joy and beauty are free in our world, and the only price we pay for respect, is compassion. It's all a matter of perspective, enjoy the journey within and the path becomes a wonderful adventure.

The angels of earth will always wonder in awe of humanities ignorance and determination. With an open heart the path is crystal clear, greed hastens self-destruction, and love and compassion always pave the way for success in life. Money is merely the confetti of success. Its importance is only worth the paper it is printed on in the bigger picture. The spear of destiny is found in the heart of mankind. To have control of your destiny, you must have your eyes focused on the destination of the journey. The greedy men will create the world they deserve: troubles, woes, and all while the rest of us continuously live in laughter, with compassion in our hearts and love in our thoughts. The secret of the universe is that life is the evolutionary transformation of energy, and compassion is the conduit of our love.

~ Love is the Yang of life's Yin's, or the answer to life's sins.

Proper attitude is dominant in our perspective of life. Our compass points north to another heart. The receptacle of love is the south pole of acceptance, this completing the circle and cycle of life. Sorrow only creates more room as it empties an infinite cup that was intended to hold love and compassion. Unfortunately, even though anger is a divisional factor of our thoughts and emotions, sometimes people let it run an uncontrolled course in their ego. When we intentionally think joyful thoughts, our path exponentially grows with compassion and inspiration. Joy lasts for the duration of life because it is found within, as the result of thought, and not the result of an action. No movement is required to find joy. It is always found in our thoughts, and is the result of thought. Happiness is the result of our actions. A Blissful life is only found when both are present in our path. Use Joy as the compass of your journey. When we close our minds to other perspectives and possibilities, we find ourselves blinded by the ignorance and arrogance of our Ego.

The reality and values of life are found in the experiencing of it, and the positive changes we can make in it. The value of our Ego or character; is our ability to take the punches thrown at us, and keep smiling as we take them. Or preferably, dodge them with a wide perspective of the situation, and a little alchemy of our thoughts and emotions. The major lesson of life besides learning how to share love and compassion is learning to coexist without passing your personal judgment on others, and that requires discussions that are nonjudgmental due to our personal perspectives.

Communication is wonderful until it turns into persecutions, due to ignorance. Sometimes our flaws give us our beauty and character, but sometimes also they define it. The trick is to discover your flaws, so you can deal with them. The value of friendship is priceless in life. Friends are the glue of sanity; they are the Sun on a rainy day. Friends are the melody in the song of life. The more you have the happier and more joyful your life is.

The Avatars

We are all Avatars of our own environments. The freewill and determination that we show as effort for a cause, is a spark of inspiration for others to follow. A wasted thought is a shame. But a wasted cause is a crime in the efforts of our universal cosmic design. Make an effort to play the game, everything appears for a reason. It's your job to decipher its purpose.

Thinking of the game of Domino's relative to life, the enlightening perspective of one, can cause a chain reaction effecting, this changing the perspective of us all. By accepting our naturally peaceful perspective, we can find peace in humanity. Who wants to play? Oops we already are. =o)

We are all unrealized Avatars of our existence, only when humanity discovers the truth in creation, and can harness the directional flow of our personal energies as a society, will humanity complete its conscious evolution and find a content society within its environments. Until we can individually accept the unity of coexistence in life as a whole, and acknowledge the need for our positive thoughts within society, there will be disputes between people and countries, caused by our feelings of ownership, pride, greed, lust, discontent, anger, and self-righteousness.

When our children can understand that the power of a positive perspective and attitude is omnipotent during the journey of life, is when society will fully understand the value of teaching love and compassion to them in school, as well as in the home. It is not only the parent's job to enforce proper conduct, but everyone's in society. Children are influenced by their peers, and others adults, almost more than their parents. Therefore, as humans in society, we should set a good example as a society, and not just at home. The beauty, joy, and compassion of life is found in our hearts first, and then in our thoughts of others. Due to the process of Cymatics, the whole cannot be greater than the sum of its parts. Therefore society and humanity will never be any greater than the attitudes, and perspectives, of our children, as well as the adults, because they are3 next in line.

In the task of transformation, you must start with yourself, and then work outwards to those around you. In the task of evolution, you must start by teaching the children because they are the ones that take our place. Those of conscious maturity are able to make proper choices concerning the future once they are shown the past, and given the present options. However, sometimes the less mature, like to experiment with the unknown in their attempts to find knowledge, profit, adventure, and entertainment. This may lead to uneducated conclusions and habits, if not properly guided. When we as parents and adults of society, learn to teach our children of the community, that life is not about what I want, but what we as the society called humanity, all living on the entity called Gaia need, is when the world will be at peace with itself, and everything else.

We are all Avatars of our children, and they grow up with the attitude we show them in society in the back of their mind. Our rights are based on our humanity and religion, as well as our personal perspectives of laws, and individual cultures. Humanity has an obligation to responsibly respect all of our basic human rights. As humans living in a society, we are responsible for defending each other's rights, freedoms, beliefs, and the right to a personal opinion. We are also responsible as a group for the health of society as a whole. This includes mental health and truthful knowledge. If one person gets ill and has no care, then the rest may fall to the illness as well.

As with life, quantum physics, and with relativity to motion, a thought true or false, and an infection, has the tendency to spread to the areas around it. We are all part of one entity coexisting in separate vessels. Our lives are the blood of humanity's existence.

We are all responsible for each other's reality, while we journey through the capillaries and veins of our human society.

When we as a society can work together as a whole entity, is when humanity will no longer be blinded to the individual needs of its people and parts. I find it odd that it takes a tragedy most of the time to bring people together, and care for each other with compassion. This should be felt and projected every day. A simple howdy, or hi to the person walking down the street can change your, and their attitude, even if it's just for the moment. To proceed in a progressive way, we must create the proper perspective, and then a better day, by laying the foundation for it. Whether you enjoy the journey or not, it is what you make of it.

We must not conceal from ourselves that no improvement in the present depressing situation is possible without a severe struggle; for the handful of those who are really determined to do something is minute in comparison with the mass of the lukewarm and the misguided. (Albert Einstein, 1934)

Have you ever thought about what thoughts are made of?

Could thoughts be waves?

Is it possible that our thoughts create waves of energy that can transfer to external matter? I believe that thoughts transfer information in waves of energy, and therefore have a frequency. Thus, they contain information that can be transferred through the standing waves in space. Of course, one would have to have enough mental energy and intelligence to have an effect on anything physically. But this would allow for a single consciousness to pick up, or transmit thoughts to other conscious minds. Although the method of reception would be purely conscience based. Theoretically they could affect Matter in a physical way, and this would explain any possibility of **Telepathy,** or **Telekinesis.**

If we think about a **chameleon,** and how it changes its *pigment to match its surrounding environment,* does it have enough intelligence to visually see and determine what color its surroundings are and match? Or, is it more plausible to think the (suit of its consciousness) is simply absorbing, and reflecting the frequency of its surroundings.

Synesthesia:

Synesthesia: Is the involuntary joining of two senses, a meeting of thought waves or some common thought processes, information of one sense is accompanied by the perception of another sense. In addition to being involuntary, this additional perception is regarded as real to the individual, and often being perceived as outside the body, instead of imagined in the mind's eye.

Do we all have some synesthetic abilities?

Synesthesia abilities are abundant. In studies done with two shapes, One a Star-burst, and the other is an Ink splash. Both were given a name, One of them Booba, and the other Kiki. Which Name would you give to each object?   Think about it for a moment. Now decide which name you would give them individually. We'll come back to the answer.

The point is that people have the same thought process, and it is based on sounds, shapes, and the waveform of our thinking process, being unified in origin and purpose. *According to* Kohler's study, 95% to 98% of people choose Kiki for the orange angular shape, and Booba for the rounded shape. "Perhaps that is because the curves of the amoeba like figure mimic the fluidity of the sound `booba', and subconsciously we reproduce the vibrational motion with our lips as they produce the smooth`booba' sound, and softer blue tone. On the other hand, the sound `kiki' and the crisp sounds it mimics, relates to the sharp edges of the crisp orange visual shape.

The only thing the two senses have in common is the TPO gland and gene. It has been found that people with damage to the left side of the parietal lobe, lose the booba-kiki ability effect. They cannot match the shape with the correct sound. This is relative to the signals from the brain being disrupted or distorted by the physical brain and its senses during communication with our spiritual mind. This leads me to the fact that aside from my wish to correlate our subconscious thought patterns of humanity, it really doesn't matter because, we are all perfect just the way we are, and we all have our individual purpose to fulfill within life, and we were given the tools we need to complete our grander purpose in life. Occasionally finding our purpose in the chaos of reality isn't the easiest thing to do. But, with peace of mind, and balance in our thoughts, we can find the answers to all our questions, systematically.

Forgive as you live. When you forgive someone and carry a grudge, you are only hurting yourself and lying to your friends. To forgive means to let go of, but to do this, you must find a way to personally understand the reason for your pain, or disrespect.

We can only let go of something by understanding it, and then accepting it. Therefore you must have the courage to look inside and let go, before you can honestly forgive yourself or someone else. Only when one journey ends, does another begin. Thus, to be able to move on within a relationship, you must first forgive those you care for, otherwise tensions builds causing a lack of mutual respect, and then if there is still no communication, or forgiveness. The relationship will deteriorate due to lack of a bond. When we forgive others or our self for a mistake or poor choice in thought or action, we get to empty our cup of emotions and regret, so that it may be filled with the knowledge of the next task and lesson.

The only thing standing in the way of cause and effect is the proper process. Sometimes we need to go with the flow of energy, and then adjust our sails and heading when we come to a reef. We are currently hung up on a reef in society because people refuse to adjust their sails to a different angle of wind. Life is full of reefs, although you never truly know until you get there if your keel will pass over; the energy of the wind pushes us through time without fail. Our reefs are the hidden adventures, pleasures, and dangers that are unseen from the surface until you are upon them. They are the tides of life and unavoidable. Therefore, one must navigate with a proper attitude, to a heading of a positive and beneficial course, to gain ground toward a beneficial and positive future.

Focus on the journey and the direction, not the surface of your path. Your smooth sailing or rough seas are relevant and proportionate to the difficulty of your task. This is known as the effort it takes to reach your goals, and it varies in degrees relevant to your choices along the path. I understand that in the fight for humanity, and our choices sometimes take us to places that others aren't ready to accept the reality of, but i do want to say, for those who can't accept what humanity is, it's differences, Multicultural benefits, individual perspectives, controllable emotions, and lifestyles, they will never be able to understand who people are, and why they do the things they do.

To truly understand humanity, we must look, and venture into all depths and beauties of it without prejudice. Then while we are there, we can spread a positive attitude and perspective from inside the circle of friendship, this benefitting our whole society if done properly. Within the harmonious frequencies of life and thought we can find the place in our mind known as the inner self. To find the reflection of ones peace of mind is the soul's quest, within the form of our physical presence. We are merely reflections of our thoughts. Thus, we create the environment we exist in. The real task at hand is the realization of our true destiny, and the acknowledgment that we are all on the same journey with equal value. We must quest to leave the world a better place after we have gone. This because if not, our children will be the ones left holding the bag as the saying goes.

'PACK OUT YOUR TRASH '

For those who know it's time to share, because those who are ignorant need to be enlightened. Have a blessed journey down the path you choose, every action you make both reflects, and affects something, or someone else as well as yourself. Let the light of joy in your life be bright. Peace and logic are the only way to solve problems. Let's all come together and figure this out before it's too late to fix. In life communication is important to pass ideas and ideals. Everyone sees life from their own perspective, only when knowledge is shared, do we find understanding in other perspectives. When we can understand the perspective of others, we can find balance in cause, and progress in a fruitful direction for everyone. If we fail to communicate our point, then we fail at making our point. Reality is found in the balance of truth and perception.

I believe the woman has the power to affect male attitude and perspective on a daily basis. So for all you beautiful women out there, be kind. Let's focus on the greater attitude and perspective, enjoying the beauty in life that we create as a team, while passing our compassion and respect to those we encounter. In the process we can do our part, to protect and admire the being of our promised devotion, and inspire compassion and equality to others. I guess that means the attitude of the world, is really in your hands in a way, decent men only aim to please those we love. Be gentle.~<3~

~ The moment we give up, is the moment we stop caring. To finish strong, we must finish the task. Whether it is opening a door or completing a building. We need to carry through in completing our goal. Each step forward is required, for the next step to appear.

Never give up. Because, if you do, then you're done.

The Consistency and Structure of Substance Within Life

As Bertrand Russel wrote. "We all start from a naive realism, i.e. the doctrine that thing are what they seem, We think the Grass is Green, That stones are hard, and that snow is cold. But, Physics assures us that the greenness of the grass, the hardness of the stones, and the coldness of the snow, Are not the greenness, hardness, and coldness that we know in our own experience, but something very different. The observer, when he seems to himself to be observing a stone, is really, if physics is to believed, observing the effects of the stone upon himself.' Bertrand Russel

Our consciousness is separate from our body, yet contained in our mind. Our conscious thoughts control our mind while awake, allowing us to give directions to our body through our thoughts. The mind may be affected physically or chemically limiting our ability to communicate with the rest of our body, but our spiritual consciousness is unaffected. A person may be mentally or physically handicapped and not able to communicate or move properly. But, this does not mean that his/her consciousness is any less intelligent then yours or mine. Only that their brain is distorting the information coming from their conscious mind, before it travels to their body, this disrupting the proper actions and movements within their physical world, even their speech or hearing may be affected causing great difficulty in communications due to a lack of understanding. When we die, our body loses its life force, and the process of thought. Thus, its flexibility, and ability for self-motivation is removed as well. The energy field of mass begins to decay, and slowly stops resonating frequency. At this point, the body starts to decompose. As our body's mass and structure loses its cymatic adhesion, and electromagnetic bond.

The atoms begin to corrode and return to their state of origin as smaller particles, eventually dissolving as they are recycled in the cycle of Earth. This is commonly known as decomposition, and it is the final stage of animal life. This contributing to the grand cycle of nature, and all life, our conscious thought or spirit, leaves our body to join the consciousness of the universe. Some call it Heaven, some call it the next level, and some call it the source of creation. They are all the same place, only different names and beliefs of what will happen.

To argue about belief of existence or death is illogical. We are living in the here and now, hopefully looking toward the future of our children. Therefore, we should have a common goal in mind. A common ground to work from outside of our individual belief or religion. Life and consciousness are like your VCR. Once you understand how it works, and why. You can easily adjust the time, or in Life's case, the problems of society. Don't let your ignorance turn to arrogance. Energy is energy. It's not mystical unless you choose to think of it that way. It's created by the frequency, and motions from the rest of life within space.

Just as air seeks the surface in water, air seeks the void in the, I'll say vacuum of space for now. Energy transforms with the application of motion due to the infinite frequencies and energy forces created by our thoughts. The Quarks, Partons, Bosons, and Fermions that make up Matter from space during our creation, first form a single particle in the process of solidity as we perceive it.

This is an illusion of solidity of course because as a structure has multiple parts. Just as a building is made of many studs, and types of material, your body and all Matter, is made from similar individual parts and pieces that form the facade of a solid structure in our brains, making them real to our individual minds, and thus our reality is formed through our symbiotic conscious coexistence.

The building is an illusion of solidity because the structures' definition is consistent with one pre-designed idea, but before it is the sum of its parts, it is empty between the spaces and must be assembled, just like you and me but with different skilled talents and laborers.

Frequency and the structure of Matter are built in the same fashion. A series of actions that have force and pauses that give an option for change, solid in appearance yet hollow in-between its individual parts. This gives us the individuality and differences that we see in a human character. Our Overall perspective, attitude, and energy, fills in the air gaps of our body to complete our physical being, The variations of frequency and energetic poles within our body give us our different characteristics, as well as our hormones and genes, They all complete the package of our physical body and soul. In reality, the Wave structure of Matter shows us how particles are formed with spatial spheres of resolution, created by the frequency of sound patterns formed from waves of energy within the void of space.

With cymatics and basic electricity, we can see how mass and energy fields are formed. We also discover in cymatics, why the planets rotate, and are constantly changing and expanding. cymatics, is the effect of sound on the substance of energy. Everything in our reality is made of a semi-substance that our mind perceives as solid. The bond of substance is made of the universal energy and the infinite frequencies found within the fabric of time. God would be the conductor of the universal music that we all hear and see. The energy of life is constantly in motion and transformation. The direction we apply the energy in, is relevant to our perspective of the moment. Joules for joules, the Positive energy of light, always defeats the negative energy of absence.~<3~

With basic electricity and magnetism, we know that - attracts +. If we apply this to a planet's energy field, where the objects are not connected to the planet, and accept ourselves as beings of light and energy. Being of a positive nature, and therefore we have a heavy proton/+ base nucleolus. Then we realize that the planet's nuclide's energy is neutral in its mass because of its momentum while revolving. OK, stay with me. The mass of the substance surrounding the earth is not a source of revolving gravimetric motion like the planet is. Thus, the objects with mass around the earth are attracted to the surface. This is because of the different poles of energy, and the attraction process of cymatics constantly trying to incorporate smaller objects into its structure. Don't believe me? Sit still without moving and breathing and see what you're made of in five or ten years. Odds are you will have died and decayed leaving the calcium of your body, too further decay in its due time. Now ask yourself, why does lightning come from the air, and seek the ground?

Answer moving from Air to Ground, or from a + to - position, is the normal order of natural magnetic, and electrical attraction. All mass and structure has a charge of (+ or -) due to the energy field that surrounds the atoms, this explains the attraction of gravity quite simply; weight being relative to mass and size of its structure.

In *Einstein's theories of Relativity*, The speed or motion of an object, projects it in a straight line. This is relative to the speed of travel, and strength of energy being applied by the nearest spinning mass with gravity. Planetary gravity being based on the magnetism of energy has Poles, and therefore a force of attraction, to hold the moon in orbit. The opposite is true for the sun and earth. The Sun has the larger mass and there for more magnetic pull to the Earth holding it in orbit around the sun. This, while the moon is more attracted to earth because of its proximity.

If the Earth and Moon were ever to approach the Sun, eventually the Moon would be more attracted to the Sun in the war of relativity. The relative angles and their positions north, or south of the two planets' axis's gives them a wobble in their rotations. This is also related to their seasonal equinoxes. This simply explains the creation of planets, and the evolution of the universe and life. Starting with the first particles creating a planet, and then others making up our universe, life evolved from forming particles and Matter.

Life starts in the form gas universally, and liquid individually, Then it continues to form Plasma, and finally Tissue, and Solids depending on the type of life, capable of thought and motion, or firmly bonded minerals, the mixtures of them, creating life, and reality in the world as we know it. To enjoy life, keep a positive attitude while grounded, and enjoy the journey during the lessons of your actions. Our thoughts are the energy of our substance, projecting out through our choices and actions. The infinite space of a singularity could be explained by theorizing the singularities, or black holes as doors to other dimensional universes, points of energy exchange within the cycle of life. Our physical properties of mass and substance, exchanged for new energy. This would make the other side the exact opposite in the cycle of energies transformation, or you could say, the mirror's reflection of our existence. Simple and logical if you think about it, if you have questions about the Wave Structure of Matter, cymatics, or basic Electricity and magnetism, you can google it. The videos on YouTube are great and very visual as well. You just have to sift through the bull crap to find the truth.

~ One can only lead a horse to water, we cannot make them drink. ~ But we can teach them if they wish.

Work done relative to Frequencies & shapes

Key information found Within 'The Messages from Water' By Dr Emoto. From **Mr. Emoto's** work, we are provided with factual evidence that human vibrations *of energy, thoughts, words, ideas and music, affect the molecular structure of water*. Liquid Matter is the starting position of most forms of life. The quality and integrity are vitally, are important to our evolution and growth. Conscious life forms from a liquid that is affected by our thoughts, so the quality of our life is directly connected to the quality of our thoughts. Liquids' physical shape easily adapts to whatever environment it exists in. But its physical appearance is not the only thing that changes, the molecular shape may also change.

The energy, or *vibrations of the environment, will change the molecular shape of liquids*. Therefore, liquid not only has the ability to visually reflect the environment. But, it also molecularly *reflects our environment. Mr. Emoto* has been visually documenting these molecular changes in water by means of his photographic techniques. He freezes droplets of water and then examines them under a dark field microscope that has photographic capabilities. His work clearly shows the diversity in the molecular structure of water, and the effects that our thoughts and frequencies have within our individual environments. By his experiments on waters molecular structure, we can clearly see that indeed, thoughts and frequencies affect the cymatics of ice formations, and therefore can manipulate and deform existing Matter.

Mr. Emoto has found incredible information about the effects of thoughts on water. He has also discovered many other fascinating differences within the frozen structures of water. The water from a clean mountain stream shows some beautifully formed geometric designs in their patterns. The polluted and toxic water shows grossly distorted and randomly formed structures and shapes. Thoughts and Words Affect Water, After seeing how water reacted to the different environmental conditions of pollution and music, to name a couple. *Mr. Emoto* and his colleagues decided to see how thoughts and words would affect the formation of untreated and distilled water crystals. Using words of emotions and the names of deceased persons typed onto a piece of paper, he then taped them to a glass bottle overnight.

The water was then frozen and photographed. Through this process **Dr. Emoto** has shown us the power of life's vibrations on water. Now when we take the next step and bring this transformation into reality with quantum physics, we can determine that the Matter of our substance is affected by the thoughts and needs of the whole environment. Thus, our conscious and subconscious thoughts form from the substance, or lack of substance, from our needs and desires. **Dr. Emoto** based his work on cultural science instead of natural science. Traditional science with conventional reasoning wasn't enough to enter the world of reality and religion. He used a vibration machine called an **MRA**.

By using this machine, he transferred vibrational information of a controlled environment onto the molecular structure of water, the positively energized water was then returned to its original life giving and moisturizing state, allowing for maximum moisture absorption into the cells of humans, pets, and plants, and this was then called HADO water. **HADO** water is possibly a major benefit to the healing, and maintenance of our health and vitality. With it, many symptoms of human illness were healed. There were over 10,000 people treated, that had actually benefitted. It was hard for people to accept that water could heal, and later more studies were done.

Mr. Emoto realized his idea through the observation of snowflakes. They never form the same shape. Let's stop and think about this for a second.

"Knowing that waves transfer the frequency that forms the structure of Matter, could it be that while the snowflake is forming, that the information traveling to the molecules gets distorted by the vibrations and thoughts within the local atmosphere and environment while the ice is forming? This causing the infinite shapes, I personally believe this to be true. What say you? ~ Back to **Dr Emotos** experiments.

The water is collected and then activated by aggravation. Then separated and 50 samples each taken and placed in a freezer at -25 degrees' Centigrade. These are examined in a lab kept at -5 C while being studied under the micro scope. Curiously, only a few out of the 50 samples show a crystal formation under the microscope. This might have something to do with quantum physics and the double slit experiment, where Particles and Electrons are shot through a solid surface with a double slit, and then the photons reacting as waves, create two separate patterns. But while being observed at the molecular level individually through a microscope,

They act as solid matter and pass through only one of the slits at a time, unfortunately revealing that because we are observing things, they may not act the way they do in nature. This unfortunately for science is a paradox in itself, and makes experimentation and proof more difficult to validate. What we know by experiments on water with repeated confirming results, is that water crystals grow 3 dimensionally, and thus melt the same way, from the center core out.

A lateral view reveals this. If you're at home and thinking ice melts from the outside first, Remember that is a perspective of size, and we are talking about it at the molecular level. As heat transfers through the outer layer, the effect is felt in the center of the molecules first on the outer layer. As the rise in temperature causes the ice at the center of the molecule to melt, the resonating vibrations within the wave structure of Matter causes the liquid to be forced out of the outer molecules crystalline structure of the still frozen matters tiny holes, these are found within the molecules off the ice. This also works in reverse, and appears visually to freeze from the outside first. But in fact, freezes from the inside of the molecule first, and then moves out this causing the frozen liquid to freeze first on the surface exposed to the cold temperature, and then transferring to the inside liquid effectively freezing it last.

From the center of the Matters sphere out, just like a particle would receive an incoming wave signal of vibrational frequency, and then transmit the instructions of Matter out to form the structure, and its state of Matter. Have you ever noticed how positive music lifts your spirits, and gives you energy? This is due to changing the vibrations and frequencies of your thoughts and environment. The reverse also works with sad and aggressive music. The vibrations we surround ourselves with have a direct impact on our attitude and perspective Yin or Yang our thoughts. I don't think there is any need to comment on the TV shows we watch. We all know the effect of that as seen in the minds and reactions of our children. Caution and direction is usually required.

Dr. Emotos work is a wonderful discovery that can change not only our own perceptions, but those of the world we live in as well. We now have profound evidence that we can positively heal and transform ourselves, as well as our planet. Proof the future is directly related to how we think of each other, even before we act. We can better the world simply by choosing the thoughts we think, and finding ways in which we can use our thoughts to benefit the future.

Since our environmental reality is affected by our consciousness itself, we can control how we correct, or change our thoughts to benefit humanity, instead of tear it apart by pulling it in different directions. The answer to strife and discontentment is by creating positive thoughts, actions, and words. If we all focus on a positive environment and take into account the reality of quantum physics, then we could logically conclude that the effect of a positive attitude and perspective would be a beneficial and prosperous one, not only for the environment, but for us all.

The things we see in our children today are a sign that the majority of us, have the wrong perspective of life, and that we are not appreciating the power of pre-thought, that we were given to aide us in our evolution. What happens within us will create what happens outside of us, one way or another.

Philosophy and Truth, the Theology of Religion

What is Theology of religion?

1. The study of religion, and faith, the belief pertaining to God and his relationship to our universe.

2. A vast perspective of different theological and theoretical opinions, the theoretical study of religion, and a greater consciousness, or God, Man, Beliefs, and our Morals.

There are two kinds of theologies.

1) *Natural* - The study of knowledge based on logic alone.

2) *Sacred* - The use of reason, enlightened by knowledge, the faith of seeking understanding.

The Definition of Religion = To bind strongly

1) The study of a belief in a cause of purpose in our natural existence usually involving a moral code.

2) A Man's belief in a relationship with God and all that it implies.

Man has the internal thirst, or a need to believe in a greater being. I believe this is because we all need to believe that we are part of something more than just ourselves. This is actually the truth, and we all have known it for years. Only we have not realized that we are truly all one entity and interconnected. By looking at the **bigger picture,** and taking into account the knowledge that we now have of our physical environment, and then applying a little common sense, intelligence, and logic. We can determine scientifically, that we are all part of one living entity that we call the universe.

Man as an intelligent species, has a thirst for knowledge and understanding; we are constantly questing for the truth. We are all made from, and have a common consciousness in our thoughts. This is one of survival, and the hope for a peaceful existence without drama from others or ourselves, and a quest for the understanding of all things. All the basic feelings we have of Happiness/Sadness, Compassion/Revenge, Joy/Jealousy, Love/Hate. These are all natural and controllable feelings.

We control our thoughts, therefore our actions and moods. Man can see a deeper reality then most life, because of our intelligence to understand it. (On Earth anyway). True religion is based on man's individual spirituality and beliefs. So believe this, we are all one-entity with individual thoughts, coexisting in a larger being, with his consciousness and energy supplying the current for all life, and its further creation. We all have lessons to learn, but we share a common existence in the cycle of life. In other words, we are all interconnected as one entity within the universe, and we are viewing this universe in our mind as we can individually comprehend, and understand it.

Errors in our thought.

1) *Greed* = The want for more than we personally need.

(I.e., the thought that one can never have enough money.)

2) *Materialism* = Only stuff matters,

3) *Agnosticism* = The doubt in spiritual belief.

4) *Scientism* = Arrogant belief of science alone.

5) **Competitiveness** = The urge to be better then the next person.

Theologians are no more equipped to answer the question of religion, than the scientists are. Scientists haven't been able to prove the existence, or nonexistence of God. Yet, faith and belief have come through in ways science can't explain and theologists can only theorize about. Quantum physics for some is unfathomable. This because they think it is impossible or improbable. Yet, the belief in religion alone is usually unfathomable to scientists being based on pure faith. Well now science has explained it in a very simple way that we can all understand. But we must use our intelligence, Logic, and common knowledge, to put it together. It leaves scientists with one question? What started the big Bang? This is equivalent to, what started the first sound in space that started all of our creation? For this we must believe in the faith of our own intelligence, and our common sense and logic as well as science.

We are all connected in a living and reproducing entity that has an intelligent consciousness to direct the formation of 'composite particles' from the unspecific compositions of 'fundamental particles'. This is required to form the molecules that form Matter. Matter is continuously giving off new frequency and energy, thus, has the ability for growth in life given the right circumstances. We could relate all life to our body taking in Oxygen and energy, and then giving off waste and effects. Energy is never ending and continues on infinitely, through the replenishment of the new physical lives that are constantly growing and dying. Therefore, we must consider that a greater consciousness is responsible for the process and cycles of the universe. This we all like to call God.

This is the only logical conclusion for the waves, and composite particles to be created in the pure emptiness and motionlessness of space that had to exist before all substance. The energy and thought waves behind the 'elemental particles' of Matter form and create the 'composite particles' that form the molecules forming the Atoms in Matter, the process forms the electrical energy field of life that we can feel and electrically detect as body temperature and pulse. These are part of the life force that binds us as individual entities.

This rate and frequency is relatively determined by the greater consciousness at our time of conception, and then regulated by our actions, relative to our health in our physical reality. The need for intelligence to create and process the actions of fundamental particles at the quantum level of creation implies a logical subconscious level of control, creating life in a systematic process. Thoughts are information waves of frequency that create fundamental particles. Picture the greater consciousness as the traffic director of the universe. Every civilization has had a religion to unite them and bring a common belief and system of morals to their society.

This is an instinctive urge for man to belief in something greater then himself. Yet, man is intelligent and rational. Therefore, we are capable of going past our senses, urges, and passions allowing us to transcend our current level of knowledge, and previously incorrectly learned beliefs towards society as of late.

This giving us the freewill to choose which path we take in life. Theoretically, each step you take forward, is for the benefit or destruction of mankind, and the consequently our universe. This putting your part of the world, this *being your portion of the* environment, squarely into your hands. We are each responsible for making the world a better place.

Only through positive actions toward other humans, as well as **all other life,** can we accomplish this.

The question that some people have asked, are we really living in a hologram? Can be answered with, only if you want to belief that. We are always the observers in science. We always perceive something as a reflection of what is there, or after the act of an action. So we are limited by what is ultimately coming into the human brains available senses. We are able to see what we're doing, but only as we do it. Prior to our actions, life is only a thought waiting for a reaction. It is conceivable that this is all an illusion, and that in fact, *there is nothing out there, other than what we imagine in our consciousness.*

We only see what is in our view. Thus, our individual realty is what we perceive it to be individually, but relative to everyone else's perspective as well. Since our bodies are bonded together by independent electrical energy fields, we are surrounded by a frequency of our *life's energy, or (a life force and conciseness of soul*). We must conclude that it is our intelligence that controls our physical movement, and that our perspective controls our physical state, through our thoughts and actions. This causing the effects in our environment, and allows our freewill of choice and determination to make the decisions that we act on as we affect our environment. Again, this is limited and influenced by the infinite alternative perspectives, and realities of the other intelligent beings within our environment. This is what creates the base for our common perspectives in our common reality. Is there a difference in how the world feels to us or how it really is?

~ Within the mechanics of quantum physics is the answer to that question. And the answer is Yes, definitely. Our conscious life is based on this, and the things we have been taught to believe through our life are because of it. The subconscious mind of our soul is in control of our reality, while our ego controls the conscious time of our limited physical life, our mind is always in an altered state while we are awake, because our senses are subject to mental, chemical, and physical distortions. The only true reality is the one in our mind, before it's affected, or infected by our senses.

Types of Matter

There are actually eight states of Matter. These are:

1 Liquid = Spaced apart.

2 Solid = Tightly packed together.

3 Gas = The neutral medium, being part of both liquid and solid.

4 Plasma = A mixture of particles and energy fields.

5 Bose-Einstein Condensate: A New Form of Matter, The atoms within the condensate obey the laws of quantum physics and are as close to absolute zero—minus 273.15 Celsius or minus 459.67 degrees Fahrenheit—as the laws of physics will allow. Physicists related it to an ice crystal forming in cold water.

6 Fermionic condensates' = They travel in waves, or more specifically the structure of a wave, They define composite particles. The gap between the everyday world of life, and the Micro-domain of quantum physics.

7 A Quark-gluon plasma (QGP) or a (quark soup) = A phase of quantum chromodynamics (OCD) Which exists at extremely high temperatures and/or densities. It contains almost all free moving quarks and gluon's, which are some of the basic building blocks of particles.

8 Tissue = *This is what we are made of, A flexible substance with an energy charge running through and around it allowing for motion in animals and other living creatures. A mixture of Plasma and Solid, a fermion based type of Matter.* If you include intelligence in this tissue, you get a growing mass that is controlled by our conscious intelligence.

Matter can change form in a few ways.

By *evaporation, condensation, thermal destruction, irradiation, sonic disruption, energy pulsation, and combustion.*

~ **Evaporation:** *Liquid changes to gas.* **Condensation:** *Gas changes to liquid.*

~ **Thermal Destruction:** Denser **solid Matter,** *Is heated until it burns and forms a **less dense** Matter that we call Ash.*

~ *Irradiation: By excessive light waves of a distorting frequency mutation of Matter occurs.*

~ **Sonic disruption:** *Powerful bursts of a specific frequency are applied forcing the disruption of the molecular bond by intensive vibrations.*

~ **Energy pulsation:** *High voltage plasma or electricity is used to fuse Matter together. (similar to welding)*

~ **Combustion:** *Through a radical change in the **frequency waves,** Matter is separated from its structure causing parts of its original structure to return to their **neutral state of existence.***

Tissue and Temperature

The living bodies of all animals consist of three types of Matter. Tissue, Liquid, and Solid, this combination of Matter forms living and conscious life. Tissue Matter is a combination of Plasma, and Solid Matter. This allows the movement of thought, light, and energy within our body. All structures are made of Atoms, and their parts, at the quantum level. We have learned that when Matter forms structure, the electrons and protons form an energy field (or orbit) around the mass and structure. We have also learned that electrons and protons accelerate when they are exited.

These exited electrons and protons move faster, and therefore produce more heat. Liquid is the first form of Matter to form structure in the body, and it then continues to grow as Tissue forms, Then solid bones begin to form giving our bodies a mobile structure. They remain somewhat pliable until the calcium has built up enough to make them rigid. Usually 7-10 years I would guess by the age children start getting broken bones more easily from accidents. And that is really just a theory of mine. I have no official statistics only my experience from childhood and parenthood. The heart pumps the blood through the body causing motion and also energy, this charging our structures energy field and allowing us to move. The more mental energy we can create, the faster and stronger we are. When the heart beats faster, and when we feel ill due to an infection or something, this causes the Electrons and Protons to move faster, effectively raising our temperature slightly.

Static shock is a quick transfer of energy that we receive from build up the excited protons and electrons in the mass of another structure. This explains why it doesn't have to be an electrically conductive material to transfer statistic energy. Static electricity is formed at the smaller scale of our normally used electricity. There are four types of energy that I can describe, plus variations thereof. The first type is what we call electricity, and it powers our homes. The second is static electricity, and it builds up when electrons and protons are exited around a structure. The third is the natural energy found in our body, also known as your Chi. It is the pure energy created and drawn upon between your thoughts and body, it's also relevant to the planet's energy force, while in the planets field of energy. The fourth type is your thought energy, or the power behind our thoughts. This allows us to think and process the information we gather, it is basically our life force of existence even when we are away from our body. It also controls the link between our Chi, and physical actions.

Some energy may have different effects on different planets, depending on their relative individual energy fields but that is speculation. All structures have an energy field of some magnitude. Our physical energy is regenerated by the frequency of our heart beat. The EKG readout at the doctor's office is simply the rate, and amplitude, of your body's energy field or, our physical frequency of energy waves passing through a conductive and monitored conduit or wire.

Our body is the vessel for our conscious knowledge and intelligence. The brain is the control point of our conscious knowledge this is why brain damage and mind-altering drugs affect learning, memory, and the physical thought processes as it passes through our physical brain. Yet, our intelligence is kept but limited in our physical usage. Our brain processes our intelligence between the body and mind. A more accurate term for our mind would be our consciousness. Just because one can't move their fingers or speak, doesn't mean they don't want to. For this reason humanity consists of how we think of and treat each other, not just how we help each other when it's needed.

True compassion is found in the mind, not in the action. *But, both are needed to make a real difference in our reality.* Some of us were taught in Sunday school that GOD spoke life into existence. We now have the knowledge of frequency transferal, and can conclude that waves of frequency began the creation process of mass and life. This by the transmission and direction of thought waves and energy, this was most likely created by the greater consciousness as the conductor of life's symphony. Life does originate from frequency and motion in space, and this is powered by the Matter and Antimatter particles of life being exchanged by the black holes of our universe and dimension during the process of our exchange of energy while refueling with the other universes and dimensions.

All this happens within the body called God that we all exist in. We can acknowledge that the universe is a large body of space, and that we are all connected in it by the vibrations of frequency that create energy itself. We also have to acknowledge that a living, growing, and moving body, must have intelligence to exist in our reality. Then we can conclude that what we call GOD is the consciousness of the universe. The word God probably spoke was actually a thought of growth, and the energy, or amplitude and frequency of his thoughts created mass, and structure from the movement and direction of the original fundamental, and subatomic particles that cause structure to form definition, and this creating the composite particles of physical life, then those particles create the mass and structures of the energy fields that exist within our space.

We as a collective intelligence view our reality as our life in the environment. Therefore, we can again conclude that GOD is in all things, and that he or she is responsible for all life in the universe. He may possibly consciously affect our reality, but only in ways that our minds can accept and comprehend. It is doubtful that GOD pays attention consciously to an individual, unless attention has been drawn to him, her, or it through some distracting or powerful thought of energy. Kind of the way we find out about cancer. Always a hidden thought until it is revealed as an issue.

Think of a Spider web, Life makes up the web, and the wind is blowing, How do you tell the spider something is in its web? You have to make an effect, large enough to overcome the common vibrations.

"Everything that the human race has done and thought is concerned with the satisfaction of deeply felt needs and the assuagement of pain."-Einstein

The Tree of Knowledge, In the Book of Genesis:

The tree of knowledge, and occasionally translated as, the tree of conscience. Was a tree in the middle of the Garden of Eden. God directly forbade Adam (Eve having not yet been created) to eat the fruit of the tree. A serpent later tempted Eve, Who was unaware of the prohibition to eat the forbidden fruit. The serpent had suggested to Eve that eating the fruit would make one wise. Eve and then Adam ate the forbidden fruit, and they became aware of their nakedness. After this, in order to deny them access to the tree of life (and, hence, immortality), God banished the couple from the garden, obliging them to survive through agriculture "by the sweat of [their] brow" **(Genesis 3).**

God set a guard about the garden to protect the tree of life from Adam, Eve, and their descendants. Thus, the knowledge that one's consciousness lives on was hidden.

Is the guard our own Ego? Are we unwilling to accept the truth until we are ready to move up to the realization that we are all one entity, with separate consciousness. We were born from dust to experience life, and complete the circle of existence within a greater entity before our body returns to dust, and this adding energy and process, to the necessary cycle of life. The constant transformation of energy occurs with our use of it within the reality of the universal mechanics, and cycle of life.

'A great mind is not constrained by specialization.'
Albert Einstein's genius illuminated religion, politics, and education as well as science.

Einstein's theory of religion puts things into perspective.

~ All life makes up our own fears through imagination, thus creating the end result of fear in reality. With primitive man it is above all fear that evokes religious notions, fear of hunger, wild beasts, sickness, death. Since at this stage of existence understanding of causal connections is usually poorly developed, the human mind creates illusory beings more or less analogous to itself on whose wills and actions these fearful happenings depend. (Albert Einstein)

Christianity, Hinduism, Atheism, Bahai, Taoism, Jainism, Buddhism, Mormon, Rastafarian, Paganism, Wiccans, Druids, Odinists, Shamans, and Sacred Ecologistsm With all the different perspectives on life and religion, unless we all come to a common belief in the truth of reality, there can be no agreement from any single perspective due to so many interpretations of the truth. The truth is we are all made from a common substance and therefore we are all interconnected. To dispute the name and practice of our belief is illogical. We are all worshiping the energy force of life, the greater consciousness that we subconsciously, all know to exist.

From the online dictionary wikipedia encyclopedia..

Messiah, Is the term designating a figure, and a concept central to Judaism, and Christianity. In these religions, A Faith is held that at some time in the history of humankind should appear a man to redeem the world and to make it better. Defeating the anti-Christ of evil intent. The word "Messiah" derives from the Hebrew mashach (_Ux, "anointed").

Anointed = 1 : to smear or rub with oil or an oily substance

2 a : to apply oil to as a sacred rite especially for consecration b : to choose by or as if by divine election; also : to designate as if by a ritual anointment <critics anointed the author as the bright new talent>

Question: "What is the anointing? What does it mean to be anointed?"

From the online dictionary wikipedia encyclopedia..

The New Testament Greek words for "anoint" are chrio, which means "to smear or rub with oil, and by implication to consecrate for office or religious service"; and aleipho, which means "to anoint." In Bible times, people were anointed with oil to signify God's blessing or call on that person's life.

(Exodus 29:7; Exodus 40:9; 2 Kings 9:6; Ecclesiastes 9:8; James 5:14).

A person was anointed for a special purpose, to be a king, to be a prophet, to be a builder, etc... There is nothing wrong with anointing a person with oil today. We just have to make sure that the purpose of anointing is in agreement with Scripture. Anointing should not be viewed as a "magic potion." The oil itself does not have any power. It is only God that can anoint a person for a specific purpose and the excessive oils of life. If we use oil for anointment, it is only a symbol of what God has done.

Another meaning for the word anointed is "chosen one". The Bible says that Jesus Christ was anointed by God with the Holy Spirit to spread the Good News, and free those who have been held captive by sin **(Luke 4:18-19; Acts 10:38).**

After Christ left the Earth, He left us the gift of the Holy Spirit **(John 14:16).**

With so many religions all over the world, it's easy to see how people and their beliefs can be so different. But, if you look at each religion beliefs, you'll find that they are all correct in their basis of beliefs. This because they all come from the same origin, yet they have divided into separate fragments of perspectives, because of location and language barriers, there is an overseeing consciousness, or GOD if you will that exists in all things. All life is interrelated, and interconnected. Happiness, Goodwill, Anger, Discontent, Pride and Humility, these are all just the natural feelings during the course of learning our lessons in life.

Life is the experience of one's personal consciousness. Religion is a belief of societies cultural, and moral rules, that one is supposed to live by. It's the binding thought of culture and belief. The truth in reality is that we all live by the same rules. Therefore we should try and live for the experience of life and not the spoils of life. By putting the goodwill of all into our future thoughts and creations we can change the world.

All religions have the common good of humanity in mind. We are all part of one universe, and everything in the universe is interconnected. The universe is the celestial body of our existence and there is only one overseeing intelligence per body, so again, we are all worshiping, or believing in the same thing and being, but from our own perspectives and beliefs. It's the same consciousness in the universe that forms the energy, and creates everything.

So, why all the wars? We all have, and are born with a universal understanding of right and wrong, as well as the ability to understand someone else's perspective. We are taught the bad habits of strife, hate, greed, poor ideas, and our past ideals of social status and materialistic importance. The only quarrel is over whose perspective is right. The answer is BOTH. We are individuals, with our own consciousness and beliefs. The common morals of society are really the unity of humanity, and the existence of life. Thus, the only thing that should be judged as good and evil are the choices and actions of the individual. The Earth and everything on it belongs to nobody.

The Earth was here before us, and it will be here long after we are gone. Therefore, we are only fleas on a dog's back. To argue over who owns the dog is pointless, we're only borrowing it, and time from each other and the universe.

This is what we need to accomplish for the common good of all. We all need to realize that we are all in this one common environment, and that we are all working for the common good of all mankind. That even though we may believe in different faiths, they all have value, and are all pointing to the same thing, just different parts, paths, or perspectives of it. We should step back and take a look at what we are really trying to accomplish, and then realize that if we all worked together toward and with this common belief that life would be much simpler, and we would all be much happier. The religion of reality, who, and what we are, is the only true religion of life. God follows naturally once we discover ourselves, because he is and has always has been there.

Personally, I think gratitude's definition is wrong in the dictionary. It should read: The feeling of acknowledgment from love and compassion. And Gratification should read as: The feeling we get from sharing our love and compassion for life with others. Through our Compassion, freewill, and determination, we can have more influence in our physical world of energy and frequency that we coexist in, if we were all on the same page.

There is more amplitude in our combined common thoughts, than in a single thought. We need to focus our thoughts in one general direction at a time, rather than several directions at once. Then, and only then, can we really be in tune with the universe, and working toward the common good of all life. Exponential progress would follow because we would be the team of humanity, instead of being individual players sitting on the bench.

In conclusion to religion and God, if we would all realize the truth in science and logic, then we could possibly create what one might call miracles in our reality and society. Only through unity of direction and peaceful communications can we accomplish a common goal. Reality is what we make it out to be, to argue over our different beliefs and perspectives of the journey, is illogical, and chaotic in its entirety, we may have different paths, but the destinations are ultimately the same. I have come to the conclusion that we must base our belief in the reality that there can only be one God, by any name. He or she has, and does make all things, and he intended us to figure out what, and who he or she is, by giving us enough intelligence, and allowing us the time we needed. We are all connected at a quantum level of life, and we are all part of one universal body. Yet, we have different internal locations and consciousness. Life exists as the cells of a human body, independent, yet unified. We as humans use intellect and belief to determine our reality through the choices we make in life. We can all decide to work together for the benefit of everyone, in a joint effort to improve life, or we can continue working with individual beliefs. This is kind of like work, when the boss is on vacation, Currently, nothing is getting done.

For true Unity, we need a common central belief, one that encompasses all beliefs, and focuses us all toward, putting our positive thoughts into a common direction for the benefit of all mankind and life on Earth because we want it, and because it is the path of least resistance in the cycle of life. This will have the most effect on the common good of all humanity and the future of our planet.

Is the Universe Alive??

To answer this, we have to look at the definition of life.

From Wikipedia.

Life (cf. Biota) - is a characteristic that distinguishes objects that have self-sustaining biological processes from those that do not, either because such functions have ceased (death), or because they lack such functions and are classified as "inanimate." In biology, the science of living organisms, "Life" is the condition which distinguishes active organisms from inorganic matter. This is including the capacity for growth, and functional activity before the eventual transformation preceding death.

Considering: The fact that a galaxy is self-sustaining, biological, and growing in its entirety, also that it converts energy while it gives life and frequency, and that all the galaxies' make up the universe as a whole. Then we can imagine Black holes as the focal point of inter-dimensional energies and Matters recycling point. The sum of these, make up our known space of reality within our limited three-dimensional existence. This would explain the exhaust jets, and the Hawking's energy, that is expelled from the black holes axis point(s), some only have one jet. This energy is in a pure form. Note, one has recently been called a structure due to its observed size and energy spectrum when seen through an advanced telescope.

The riptide of elemental particles and energy creates the Accretion disks that we find around black holes, and other sources of intense gravity. These are the beautiful displays of light seen as whirlpools of color and substance. The Galaxy's and Universe's presumably pass Aether as a common gas relative to their dimensional position, a change in the pitch of universal frequency, may be the only real dividing factor of our dimensions. So theoretically they would feed and support each other, while existing as part of each other in the bigger picture. Thus, we would have to conclude that Yes, The galaxies and universe's are alive, having an eventual birth and death. Yet, it is infinite and immortal as far as we can determine due infinitude of time and our short time of existence within it.

Would an ant know how long a human was? The ghost in the shell is our soul, trapped in the physical vessel of our perceived journey through our individually sensed journey, through a coexistent and symbiotic world. The compass of our life is found in our knowledge of the past, and need for future progress and results. The path is determined individually by our conscious thoughts and actions.

My theory of God and evolution: X Theory

Everything started somewhere and at some time. This is how life evolves. If you can picture your soul as a light wave or (A lazar spot on the wall), A single spot on the wall spun around in a circle fast enough becomes a continuous line. Now think of that line as representing your existence through time. Now, we are imagining this line in slow motion or stopped, in our instant of reality.

Kind of like the time elapsed pictures of cars moving on the freeway at night. Life is relevant to our perspective and time. Life's energy doesn't end, it only transforms. Therefore, we can conclude there will be some kind of existence for us after death.

What it is at this point depends on your belief.

$$0 + 1 \ * \ infinite * infinite / infinite$$

(God)(thought) (Frequency)   (life) (Perspective)

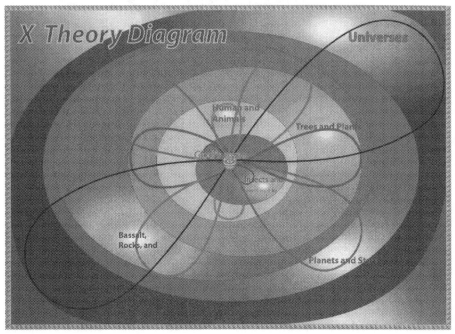

We are all one entity and ultimately connected. If you take GOD as the eye or greater consciousness existing everywhere, yet individually acknowledged and communicated with in life, and centered at the X point. Then because God is the creator of the first thought waves and frequencies in the universe, and that he supplied the energy that started everything, as well as being the breath behind its continuous flow. Then God must currently contribute to waves and vibrations that form in space, as well as the ongoing energy that is required to sustain the creation of our universe, planets, and every new individual life within it.

This process eventually evolving each galaxy, and Universe as time marches on, we are all infinity signs of different sizes, but joined at the center or the X point with our creator in spiritual consciousness. Life's path and direction are constantly advancing, but not a straight linear line. It is equivalent to an Infinity sign that is constantly vibrating due to the different frequencies we encounter, and variable decisions that we make. The X's point being our transition between birth, and death before we start another existence in Heaven, or the next plane of existence, this depends on your personal believe of course. Due to our infinite perspectives and beliefs, life is what you create it to be now and before tomorrow. Realistically tomorrow is always a day away, if we want to make an effect, we must act first, before it is recorded in or memory. Can anyone say Memorex. Just kidding.

We shouldn't think our existence will be much different in principal or process in the next phase of our existence, every reaction requires an action to start the ball rolling. Eventually, it may be the action of a concentrated thought without a physical body. But, for now we have to use our physical bodies. We are a form of conscious energy, with a subconscious illusion of solid Matter. Add in some time for evolution, and then Baaam!!, you find yourself reading a book about attitude and perspective which happens to include the explanation of your scientific existence in reality. You've undoubtedly learned a few things in the process, and hopefully have had a lot to think about to affect a positive change in your life.

~ Ghosts maybe souls who don't accept or realize that their body has ceased to function.

Personally, I think we all need to look deeper into our own minds, and explore the possibilities of people being conscious of our own self-awareness, and the consciousness of our soul, if you will. Then by concentrating that effect toward the common good of everyone, we can stop worrying about who has better dirt, or whose belief is right. We must concern ourselves more with giving our children a healthy and unified environment.

This is done by stopping our selfish and competitive ways that are taught by our past obsession of possession. We must find another source for competition, as this is really a natural urge, and can be fun. This I believe is the basis of the Olympics, to give humanity something peaceful to compete in. I'm sure there are other peaceful ways that we can find to release the negative urges we have due to being human, without doing harm to other life mentally, or physically.

But we must change our negative faults, to positive outlets of entertainment, in order to release the unwanted urges of humanity. We have to change to more positive thoughts and actions, before it's too late, and there's nothing left except a burnt up, and used planet that can no longer support itself, or any other life. This in effect would be the end of the world, solely created by humanity, with no one else to blame, but ourselves as a group because, we couldn't come together as a society to solve our selfish problems. (This thinking could be called the cancer of the planet and universe).

That would truly be a shame, because then we would all truthfully be in hell, knowing what we did as a society. It only takes a change in attitude and perspective toward life, for life to be as perfect as humanly possible. And yea that's all relevant to your perspective of what is possible.

~ Everything is transformed in the end, energy is the substance behind matter, anti-matter, and dark matter, energy is the common cause of our existence, mentally and physically, as our reality is only the result of our thoughts and senses in a universe filled and bound, by the vibrations of frequency, that we define as cymatics, this along with the electromagnetic bond that forms the life force of our energy field, (the glue of our molecules and atoms structure).

This we call quantum mechanics, and the physics of a particles creation. All life has a finite cycle of time through existence and evolution as its life force transforms physical shape through an infinite journey through time. When you have a conscious soul of thought and ability you not only evolve physically, but through life and the lessons learned mentally and thus spiritually through the mind of your soul. Only when the physical brain has convinced you that reality is worth more than your soul, is when you have been totally blinded to the purpose of life. The truth is there for all to see, if we are scared to state our opinion, then we do not have freedom of speech, and in that event, we could not call ourselves free. While prisoners of our own fear, we are kept in chains within our thoughts and reactions. Fear is the weapon of choice for those without compassion.

We exist as beings of thought and light, what we see and feel are signals from our physical body's senses. We only interact with our bodies through our thoughts, the mind is separate from the body, the body is a cymaticly formed and electromagnetically bonded energy field of molecules and energy, a symbiotic cell of Gaia that we each experience our individual realities with. ~ In Lak'ech ~<3~<3~<3~

Evolution of Ecology

Ecology is the study of a living relationship, and its interactions in the environment. This includes the Ecosystems, their direct environments, and the variable scales of ecology and evolution within our symbiotic and evolutionary stages of ecology. Biological science currently has two ideas of bacteria, Micro and Macro bacteria starts in your body as a micro-organism. Millions of bacteria occupy your body and reproduce within it, this causes the spread of infection, and virus growth leading to macro bacteria, they also evolve or mutate to different strains of illness.

Macro looks at the process of evolution from the bigger picture. The view of how it has affected us in the past, and how it can possibly affect us in the future, Micro describes the same process but in a very tiny scale. These are the basic principles of evolution and ecology. However, at the quantum scale of our existence, life evolves or mutates with direct correlation to its environment.

This happens at all levels of life relative to the environmental vibrations encountered by the existing frequency that is being affected by other frequencies, needs, or thoughts. When women are pregnant, the environment, substances ingested, and the emotions a mother may have during pregnancy all have an effect on the child being developed in some way.

This whole process of our consciousness, causing the unconscious cravings we feel through time and our evolution affect our needs, and common perspectives of reality, this influences change in our thoughts by suggestive options, some are of distorted or negative energy, and these physical suggestions or vibrations, Yin or Yang the cause and effect, are giving us a slightly new form and attitude as we progress through time. This is called evolution, the changing of our structure through a process, and due to a cause.

Evolution occurs gradually through the cycles of time. Through our intelligence and past knowledge, we can deduce that the evolutionary changes are due to our perceptions of reality, and the effects we choose to make happen in our environment. We control our daily evolution through our freewill of choice, and this directly affects the life of our physical body, relevant to the environmental situations that we expose ourselves to. We always choose our environment. So, in conclusion to evolution, we individually, yet collectively, control our own fate through our everyday choices in life. Our conscious needs and actions, affect our environment, and ultimately result in the planned or unplanned changes that affect us all.

Not only in our environments, but also eventually affecting our structures, mass, unconscious thoughts, and state of being. This is constantly effecting and altering our perspectives, attitudes, and perceived realities.

Freewill and Determinism

The debate between determinism and freewill, Is the debate of life being a mechanized universe, everything being predetermined and waiting to happen, and therefore the universe works from rules, thus, actions can be determined. In principal, if you understand the way the universe works, you can then determine what is going to happen, and that freewill is an illusion. People think of Freewill, as opposed to determinism. In that we can create our own reality by our choices, freewill, and determination.

Dilbert said: 'Do you think the chemistry of the brain controls what people do? - of course, - Then how can we blame people for their actions? - because people have the freewill to do what they choose - Are you saying that "freewill" is not part of the brain? - Of course it is, it's just part of the brain that's out there being kind of free. - So your saying the freewill part is exempt from the natural laws of physics? - Obviously, otherwise we couldn't blame people for anything they do! - Do you think the freewill part of the brain is attached or just floats nearby? - Shut up! `

This is a humorous explanation of what people think that freewill is. In reality, freewill is our ability to make a choice, and then cause an effect on our environment by taking action from our choice. The mechanism of the universe takes over from there, and allows the effect of our actions to be seen and felt by the rest of our collective conscious perspectives. In conclusion of freewill vs. Determinism, it appears once again, the answer lies in the balance of both. We as individuals, and a collective, cause an effect that changes our reality, by the scientifically determined mechanism or the universe.

Here's what they say:

'For the law neuroscience changes nothing'

`Freewill is an illusion of cognitive structure; retributive notions of criminal responsibility depend on this illusion, and if we are lucky they will give way to consequential ones, thus radically readjusting our approach to criminal justice'

"New neuroscience will change the law not by undermining, But by transforming peoples Morals, and intuitions, about freedom and responsibility."(Greene & Cohen 2004 Phil. Trans. R. Soc.)

We cannot blame individuals based solely on their actions, as their actions are usually the result of society's effects on their environments. We should therefore encourage healing in the mind and body first, rather than put them in a cage and ignore the problem that we have actually helped to create. We can always put them in a cage and throw away the key if they are just evil hearted, and not deserving or stable enough to coexist with the rest of humanity. If the world is deterministic, then everything in the future is inevitable. But, I don't think it's inevitable for everyone to say, Accidently shoot them-selves in the leg.

We all have the power of choice and freewill, it is up to the logical people to keep everyone including the theorists and mathematicians, in reality. Thinking of things at the quantum level takes a lot of imagination at first. Then having to prove our imagination with realistic evidence isn't the easiest thing to do. It's easy and natural for the human imagination, to dig into to many directions at once. This is the basic instinct and goal of our imagination, to discover and create. Without it or those who do discover and create, we would still be carrying sticks and stones, while walking to the stream to get clean.

So, for all you Theologists, Mathematicians, and unknown positive thinking, intellectual types that try to make a difference, THANK YOU. For all your contributions to reality, however, the world is ultimately responsible for itself. We, being all parts of it, and are responsible for it as a whole, each action that we make has an effect that makes a difference in some way. Knowing this, if we can each do our part, trying to understand, that everyone has their own reality, and this is a result of our individual freewill and determinism, working in a mechanical universe that is affected by everyone's chaos. Then we can determine that, it's time to change our thinking a little, and take part in making a positive future for all of us.

Personal Attractions

Humanity as individual beings, seem to have a natural attraction to things of status,   beauty, value, and items of religious Importance. Individuals are also attracted to certain frequencies or vibrations of other life forms, call it chemistry. This is why you may choose one pet over another, based on its visual appearance and the frequency of its Aura. This explains why `beauty is in the eye of the beholder', and why that ugly little dog that your neighbor has, is so friendly to, and loved buy its owners, relevant to its treatment of course. When we look at life, we see a physical body. Some see an unseen Aura that surrounds us.

This Aura is in all things, but only some of us are gifted enough to see it. Personal attraction is the individual belief of what we think is good, pleasant, and worth having. Everyone has their individual beliefs, and desires formed from our beliefs and feelings. These feelings are also formed by environmental locations, and our want for social acceptance and success. It is possible to be attracted to something or someone without wanting to possess them, or it. When people are attracted to something, someone, or some future, what they are really wanting, is to be accepted by someone else in society, or they feel a general attraction to its energy and frequency.

Some common attractions we desire are, love, security acceptance, and respect. There is also currently the greed for material items of stature. But realistically, this only shows how much money they have accumulated. How much money a person has or doesn't have, has nothing to do with their character. To be honest, sometimes the effects of money actually have a negative effect on our characters.

We can understand through science how we are all connected. Yet, we all perceive life differently. Thus, we have different values and attractions.

If you think of life from a universal perspective, and realize that we create what we desire through our imagination, choices, and actions. Then you can see that we are all responsible for creating our individual desires and environments. Thus, we are capable of creating a peaceful planet that works in unity with nature, along with having the common goal of good for all life. Some desires and needs change with priority of importance, but others are constant. Those are the ones we are working on improving. Having love, peace, and acceptance in our life is easy to accomplish with the proper social perspective. On a universal level if you think positive thoughts and act on them, the effect will be positive within your environment. If we would all work toward the same goal instead of our individual progress, then we would get things accomplished instead of unfinished.

So here is my challenge to each individual. Think of positive thoughts and co-ordinate your efforts with others seeking to do the same thing. This will at least get sections of our reality changing for the common good. Eventually, we will all be working in a unified direction to better the environment for all of humanity, and life. We spend too much effort pulling in different directions causing a loss of momentum in our progress, and this eventually tearing our self apart. We need to unify as humanity to accomplish miracles.

Fundamental Particles

The Fundamental particles are the structural information that makes a page of Matter or the **blueprints of life** if you will. They make up the components of a 'composite particle'. These composite particles shape *and form a molecule*. We can show through *frequency and sound experiments,* that the information of **Fundamental particles** (our thought energy), Travels through **the structure of spherical waves**. This allows for a universal communication method through the **frequency** of the waves in space. More than a billion Atoms can fit on the head of a pin, molecules are smaller than that, and 'composite particles' are 10 times smaller than that.

Fundamental particles in accord with the gauge theory need directions to move in a constructive manner while building the 'composite particles' of Matter. Thus, they must have a conscious intelligence to direct the fundamental particles during the process of constructing the composite particle of a molecule and Matter. Therefore, Matter must be made from thought waves having a purpose, as nothing exists in reality, that do not serve a purpose in some way within Gods life.

The elementary or fundamental particles

Fundamental particles are the effective language of the **Molecules in an Atom,** or to better picture it, the letters, and drawings on the page that is sent through your fax machine. This is transmitted by the frequency, force, and energy of and within the waves of space.

Quarks

Quarks are the method of motion that this information is written with. There are six types of them called flavors strangely: *Up and Down* (direction), *Charm and Strange* (forming 3 dimensional positions), and *Top and Bottom* (limits of a the page), these form a field of unity to base the page and information on, and they are the only elementary particles that exist in all reactions of attraction, electromagnetic, gravimetric, as well as the strong and weak magnetic attractions.

Subatomic particles

Electrons and Protons are the energy and force that drive the motion of the printing. When all of these forces come together under the right circumstances, particles and atoms are formed bringing mass into existence, and then creating more structure and size while duplicating, binding, and increasing the electromagnetic forces of energy that binds the substances together, force relative to size.

Composite particles

Bosons form the energy fields, and *Fermions,* define the size and type of paper. *Hadrons* and nuclides make up the words that the quark's motions define within the molecule's creation and alignments, forming the Atoms type of structure and mass.

Note: Fermions are unable to occupy the same space, at the same time. They form an intelligent and individually moving conscious life form. This allowing for birth and our individual growth from within a single womb, while being two, three, or more separate entities existing in the same physical location. Matter is the result of the music of a universe, conducted by God, the maestro of life originally, and then added to individually, by each and every one of us.

Dark Matter:

Dark matter may be the method of transport for the excess used energy particles, on their way to the recycling bin of the solar system, (The Black holes of the universe). Or maybe, it is the unused energy of life waiting to be drawn upon by the Maestro in the future, Perhaps. Anyway, either way it occupies more than 95% of our universe, and we can't even see it. There is really little known about Dark Matter. The fact that it is invisible, and we haven't been able to actually observe it plays a key role in this. We can only theorize, and make determinations about it.

Once we advance to the point of common space travel, we will eventually get to the truth of it, but for now, my theory is that it's the excess or waste, from our transformed energy, and it holds the opposite of our purpose in the transforming energy. It is the method of Matters motivation during its movement within our universe, to and from the Black holes of our galactic machines. The movement of this Dark Matter may be powered by gravity from the singularity or not. But, the whole theory of the process further completes the circle of life, and energy's natural transformation process on a grander scale. This being true, the universe is a semi sphere, and we are part of an even larger entity, that could theoretically be part of a larger one, and so on.

Quite a bit to take in at one moment, But we must realize that we are all truly connected to one consciousness. This larger being that we exist in, is our God. We are as much a part of him, as he is of us. If we want to keep him healthy, and our existence to continue, we need to start taking care of ourselves, and our environments.

Einstein and Newton on relativity

The development during the present century is characterized by **two** theoretical systems essentially independent of each other: the theory of **relativity** and the **quantum theory**. The **two** systems do not directly contradict each other; but they seem little adapted to fusion into one unified theory. For the time being we have to admit that we do not possess any general theoretical basis for physics which can be regarded as its logical foundation.
(Albert Einstein, 1940)

Newton realized this when he wrote:

It is inconceivable that inanimate brute matter should, without mediation of something else which is not matter, operate on and affect other matter without mutual contact. That gravity should be innate, inherent and essential to matter, so that one body may act upon another at-a-distance, through a vacuum, without the mediation of anything else by and through which their action may be conveyed from one to another, is to me so great an absurdity that I believe no man, who has in philosophical matters a competent faculty of thinking, can ever fall into it. So far I have explained the phenomena by the force of gravity, but I have not yet ascertained the cause of gravity itself. and I do not arbitrarily invent hypotheses. *(Newton. Letter to Richard Bentley 25 Feb. 1693)*

As **Newton**, and **Einstein** debated **gravity**, they missed the fact, that the medium in space, is a method of communication in a stationary system. Space is not really a vacuum, but a lack of air. Air in space, like in water, seeks escape from a confined container when exposed to an element of different atomic weight. Aether, I believe, would be classified as lighter than air element. Thus, air would spill out into it. Things move through space. Space doesn't move through things. There may, or may not be a current in space, but since space is the lightest substance we have it would take a sail of sometime to effect heavier mass.

Light and Matter, are only perceptions of our consciousness. Gravity is the result of Matters energy fields, polarity differences, and the attractions of opposite polarity. The larger the mass, and energy field, the larger the field, and effect, of attraction. As the planets move through space in the form of solid Matter, their velocity and direction give them momentum. This momentum projects them in a straight line, this line is affected by the attraction of magnetic energy fields as the planets orbit the Sun. This Sun is *also the largest mass, and energy field, within our solar system,* so they are pulled toward it. Yet, Their momentum of motion and rotation, constantly propel them forward as they orbit around the Sun. The alternating attractions of the North and South poles or energy fields, cause them to wobble during rotation, this also gives them the sine wave pasterns, and variable ecliptic angles that all the planets acquire during their orbits of the Sun.

Velocity, distance, and momentum control the strength of attraction. Thus, the further away they are, the less the attraction is, and therefore less momentum is needed to pull away, this relative to size and density of course. But, as planets only have their cymatic energy and the momentum, created during their creation and the slight vibrations of space to propel them, they will never reach a speed fast enough to break orbit from the sun, unless some impact alters their course. The reverse is also true, the *slower* an object moves in an orbit the *faster* it will return to the focal point of its orbit. Because everything including the sun is orbiting the center of the galaxy, and the galaxy is orbiting the center of the universe, the planets and galaxies will never lose momentum completely in their orbits. This is because of the sling shoot effects developed by moving objects with gravity, and magnetic attractions. Call it what you will. Energy, magnetics, or gravity, it's all part of the substance that binds us, and keeps us on the planet, this explaining the physics of motion.

~The duality in size and life is part of our human perception of existence. The universe is as complex as the body, cells within cells. Life exists in many forms and places. To an unborn child, Moms are the universe. What are we?? Energy and thought in a Bio-electromagnetically grown vessel of light electrically exchanging CO_2 for the energy found in O_2. The rate is measured by our use of motion in physical form. The value of life is given to all particles of an atom equally in science, and should be in our perspectives of life as well.

Gravity

Why does a ball fall to the earth? The wave motions tell us that a wave travels slower in a higher energy field of mass's density, where the frequency has more amplitude, this compacting the waves and generating a denser shape in the frequency and force of the wave. Thus, the waves that all things travel through are perceived to have more density in an object, or air. (Air is an object of chemistry), and therefore they move slower through it. Think of a feather falling to the ground. It has less density than most objects, so it travels through the density of the air slower then another object of similar size, this causing less speed of momentum, and therefore requiring less force to penetrate through the structure, or substance within its path. This is why the feather doesn't usually float straight down but will float back and forth, or spin depending on the type of feather you use.

At the precise point in time when an object enters, and attempts to pass through the energy field of another entity or structure. The entering entities energy field takes on weight in direct relation to its present environment. As the electrons and protons generate the energy field around its mass, they create two kinds of electricity. Let's say A and B, or sky and earth. Due to the electrical properties of Matter, and the magnetic properties of an energy field, A is attracted to B, or + is attracted to -, this creating a magnetic pull on the energy fields and structures surrounding the largest mass. This is the Earth from our current perspective and environment. The forces of gravity are monumental, yet the effect is weak at the point of contact. The greater the distance between objects, the weaker the magnetic strength of effect, or physical attraction, this is because the attraction of the whole entity is relative to mass with the force of attraction, weight or density at the point of contact.

The space between is a gravitational adjustment area until a common focal point has been determined for the individual objects in question. This is due to the equalization of the neutron and electromagnetics.

Gravity is based on the principals of electromagnetism at the quantum level of Matter, and increases it attraction relative to size, density, and structure. A greater then equal force of opposite energy is required to separate the energy field at the point(s) of contact on a planetary scale, we call this gravity. Now we can understand the true causal connection in physical reality which causes this law of gravitational attraction. (Space, mass, and environment)

The Answer to, What would happen if the Sun instantly disappeared?

The planets (or substance of matter), would instantly lose their attraction to the Sun, and carry on in a straight line with a slight pause, for a directional adjustment of their momentum. This until they encountered the next largest mass and magnetic energy field in our universe, to affect it once again, of course then you get a flurry of possible collisions with other masses before shall we say, the dust settles. Everything is relative to the type of Matter, Its constantly changing structure and magnetic energy field and the momentum or speed of its direction of travel.

The origin of mass

We learn that what appears to us as space is the result of a neutral dynamic medium consisting of waves, force, and frequency, these carrying the elemental particles of life that create the Bosons, and Fermions that contribute to the creation of substance. This occurs by a process of electromagnetic chemical bonding that creates the energy of composite particles, Atoms, and Matter. This process is done through a series of quantum fluctuations in space and time that cause the vibrations and movement of the forming the waves, and spheres of energy within the neutral medium of space, and our relative time. Picture the waves of a busy public pool of water, but three dimensionally as spheres of sound and frequency. The movements, cause the vibrations that allow the frequency of life to create the composite particles and energy, created by the motions of these wave interactions. This process forces Matter to form into a state of existence. This Matter is formed by the composite particles, and the subatomic particles of energy (electrons and protons). Once combined the Atoms and Molecules are formed. Matter is created by the formation of composite particles, from the fundamental particles of our thoughts, creating the energy of the `subatomic particles' that reinforce, and form, the energy field of the structure, as it is defined. Hadrons and Partons define each type of Atom.

The elementary particles transmitted through, and with the frequencies of space determine the type of Matter that can possibly be created, this defining its structural form and character while it is initially being formed.

These structures are bound and controlled, by the resulting energy fields. Energy of conscious life has the ability of motion and thought process, unintelligent structures or energy fields, can only grow. Through the progressive formations in the creation of mass, we can see how structure is formed and held together by the energy fields that are created during the Bonding process causing growth and duplication for its survival. This energy force is either intelligent or unintelligent depending on the composite particles environment, and the conditions in which it was created and grows in.

I think shell patterns show this best because of the visibly apparent staged growth patterns throughout their life. We can plainly see that life grows in stages of expansion. This is why a snake sheds its skin, because its mass has outgrown its protective exterior scaly tissue that is no longer flexible enough to allow for the expansion of its growth. As the snake starts to outgrow its limited expanding exterior skin, it must leave it behind as it forms the new larger scales of its structure. I could conclude that if we had scales, we would have to shed to. Unlike the snake, we get more intelligence as our natural defense in life, growing in spurts and reaching a plateau, before gravity and time start to reverse our size and shape.

Unfortunately, this forces us to deal with limited intelligence, destructive natures, and violence, due to the lack of proper knowledge and respect. Hopefully this book helps to educate the ignorant people that are seeing our self-destruction. Theft, and Violence, are NOT the answers to making a better existence for themselves or the environment around them, and this includes everyone and thing.

Interaction in Energy and Matter

Matter is derived from wave frequencies, interacting with energy to force structure and growth. This energy supplies our mind with the substance it needs for thought, our thoughts then allow us to make choices, these choices create energy pulses of information directed at individual parts to create independent, electromagnetic energy fields that are necessary for muscle movement, they also control growth and the involuntary functions of our seemingly solid, yet independent structure of organs and parts. The voids in our molecules allow the interactions of energy through the Tissue Matter of our body between the gaps of our nerve endings and functions. This allowing the intricate individual interactions of energy, to process correctly between the layers of our combined Matters structure, allowing the operation of individual components within the body's symbiotic systems without getting our wires crossed.

Of course with any damage to the nerves the main connection may be lost, and then the distortion of the body's energy field corrupts the information to and from that function to the point that the sensors of that area fail to communicate with the brain leaving that area a ghost by definition to the brain.

All Matter has energy that interacts with the composite particle's to form the nucleolus controlling the creation of the Atom, and Matter's state and density as well as its structural mass, size, and different characteristics of the individual structure being formed. Interaction of energy with the nucleolus is done by absorption. The Electrons and Protons are created by the process of a composite particles creation. This is done by the vibrations and forces of the common waves found in the space surrounding us.

This whole process is assisted by the greater consciousness to form a structure from need. This causing us to form our composite particles, from the elemental particles (or thought waves), from within the Wave structure of Matter. This effectively increasing the energy fields charge, and continuing the growth of structure and mass. This is done with an up, and down, left and right, spherical motion of the Quarks and Gluons.

This brings in the importance of the individual weight of the Atom, or the amount of energy absorbed, and expelled from the particles through the wave's motions. The weight of an atom dictates the structure, and density of the energy fields of Matter. The clearer and lighter a structure is, the smaller the amount of emulating energy, and strength of field that is given off.

The denser the structure is, the stronger the energy, that can be expelled as its resonating energy force. This energy binds the atoms' together tighter or not, depending on the interaction of protons and electrons, this relative to their charge and quantity or (vibration, and frequency), allowing for the different states of Matter, and the variable tensile strengths that we encounter in physics.

Atoms are bound together by external forces, constant waves of frequency bombarding them from all sides, causing the resonating vibrations within the subatomic particles, which creates the orbiting energy required for the fundamental particles, to form the composite particles, Atoms, and molecules adhesion, and growth. This forms the new specific frequency and energy pattern around its individual structure. The Electrons, and Protons are mixed as the atomic bond is formed from the specific resonating frequency of their common Atoms relative to their energy, weight, and polarity.

This effectively increases the magnetic energy field strength, relative to its growth in size, allowing it to intensify in size and strength, relative to its preferred density during its growth, this further defining the new frequencies structure while it is being created. This allows other Atoms to resonate at the same frequency creating the common electromagnetic bond and the growth of an energy field relative to its structure, and in direct relation to the environment and conditions it exists in, as it forms more individual mass, from substances ingested or absorbed.

Our Spherical Existence

Have you ever wondered why the planets were spherical instead of square, or some other shape? Perhaps it is due to the constant vibrations of waves within the pool of frequency and energy that envelopes the quantum space that we exist in. Constant equal force from all angles creates a sphere with any form without a structure or solidity to define it. Think of water in space. While all planets start of as a gas and then form water, substance, and gravity, the spinning process of cymatics causes spheres to form as the weight of substance is distributed evenly is space. Because all conscious life has a perspective of its own environment, we can conclude that each life is an observer in the universe.

From my perspective, an (observer or soul), is a spherical consciousness within a biomechanical suit that surrounds us. This suit has sensors to pick up different signatures, and frequencies of both nonphysical, and physical Matter, these from our surrounding environments, Sight, Sound, Touch, and Thought. These allow us to exist, and interact in our current dimension. Physics has proven that 96% of the universe is invisible to us. It contains two forces within it, Dark Matter, and Dark energy. They make up **96%** of the universe, and we are the 4% left over. This is what we can see, touch, and perceive, to be in our reality.

The American Indian's talked about 3 *miracles*

1) That anything exists at all.

2) That living things exist (*plant and animals*)

3) Living things exist that know they exist.

As human beings, we have the capacity to think and reason. We know, but we tend to forget two things. First, that we know that we are here as part of a whole, and secondly, that the first miracle, is that anything exists at all. Science has shown us that we are all one, and are formed from energy and controlled by thoughts, and perceptions. Fortunately we can now think of it in terms of reality and science. The only part left to achieve to complete the picture is your belief and understanding of the universe, and why we exist in it. We have determined that all things have formed from energy waves of frequency, and that through the transferal and transformation of information, intelligent energy particles are form during the process that we call cymatics. The reflecting particles' point then begins to define the structure of Matter.

The only question left is what started this huge chain reaction that we call life? Again, my belief has to fall back to the proof of the universe being a living entity, with the consciousness that we call God starting the first thought waves of our frequency in life, that we refer to as sound. This beginning the formation of our universe by starting the vibrations, and communications, of life's neutral medium within space; and this allowing the creation of life itself. Thus, the circle of life, and the creation of it as a whole, from the Macro, Relative, Miniature, Micro, and Quantum substances discovered within the cycles of our transforming and exchanging energy fields of life.

The cycle of life exists at many levels, but they all have basically the same process and purpose within the chaos of our reality. This is to transform, process, and reprocess the energy of life itself, as part of Gods body and structure. It's really the only logical, and scientifically explainable, explanation.

Conclusion

Space is a neutral and stationary medium that waves are constantly moving through. This forms the wave structure of Matter within a neutral space. This is the substance of space. In these waves of space is carried the fundamental particles of different types that form the composite particles of atoms, and molecules. These are the pages of information that are carried in the frequency of waves in space. Waves travel at a variable speeds relative to variable forces, and densities. The speed of the wave is considered the force of its energy.

Our Life forces Energy

LF = current (our power of our thought) / Resistance (humanities physical beliefs).

Simplified ~ Our Life Force Energy = Our thoughts and determination / Our beliefs.   ~ This is also known in electronics and electricity as I = V/R

When waves converge a particle is forced to form using the Information, energy, and vibrations of frequency that are supplied by the quantum spatial magnet energy of sub atomic Matter and Antimatter. By using dark matter as its theoretical neutral conduit and field of transportation in space to create and transfer the energy that forms mass within our reality. Mass is created through resonating particles, and energy fields, bonding during their creation.

There are 8 states of Matter; Liquid, Solid, Gas, Plasma, Bose-Einstein condensate, fermionic condensate, and Quark soup, which is a mess of pieces left over from the collisions of Matter, and Tissue, a plasma and solid combination. When a conscious energy wave, say the consciousness of the universe, directs and combines the fundamental particles that form the composite, and subatomic particles of our physical substance which in turn forms the Atoms, and Molecules of life. This process provokes particles to form an energy field around the Matter being constructed. The universal conscious forms the unintelligent energy fields that form our natural elements and their masses,(Gas, Earth, Fire, Water).   Akasha is the fifth element and the container of life.

When subconscious thought waves combine we get organic life, when intelligent conscious energy waves of physical love enter the equation, we get tissue a duplication and procreation of tissue Matter, and another intelligent energy field creating mass, and life as a sentient being. This mass resonates and strengthens, relevant to the nutrition and surrounding energy field. As growth occurs, more mass and structure is formed. All mass slowly changes form through time, and this is called evolution.

Gravity is simply the effect of the largest opposite pole of electromagnetism, relative to two energy fields, and there related mass, density, and position to each other. The strength of attraction is relative to its position, structure, and mass. Energy and magnetism cause Matter to form opposite poles of energy that react with others structures and magnetic fields due to the electromechanical properties of energy.

The earth as well as the galaxy, breathes and exchanges energy and Matter. Therefore, the universes are living entities by the definition of life. We are all interconnected through the common consciousness of creation as a substance of frequency, thought, movement, and energy. The greater consciousness and being we call God was the beginning, and is the center of all life. We as individuals have many beliefs based upon our personal perspectives, and personal environments. But if you look at what we are all worshiping and desiring, it is a peaceful world around us, including all the people and life we coexist with.

The energy of life and the greater consciousness we believe ourselves to exist in, is all around us, and flows through us all. We all believe in the same thing, only in different ways, or from different perspective. For positive and controlled progress of the human race to proceed, we as a group need to focus on one direction at a time, then something would get done. At the moment, humanities manager seems to be on vacation and the blind mice are playing their fiddles with great intent, but little progress is being made.

We have learned through our time of existence that everyone has their own perspective and belief, the problem with this is that it causes chaos in our existence. To be unified we must all have a common goal and belief. Through science and intelligence, we can determine our existence, and why we are here. What our purpose is can only be theorized upon. My thought would be to experience life before our next level of existence as we process God's energy. Our spiritual life force of energy and consciousness will never really cease to exist. We only transform into another form of being. Therefore, the journey and the mental view of life is what we must value as really important.

Not how much progress can be made, but the quality of the human progress being made. Upon death our life force, energy, and intelligence **(or soul)**, transforms from our perceived solid energy form into the reality and consciousness within the universe *(or God's consciousness)*, before we start our next level of perceived existence at the time of our choosing. Life is a repeating form of energy that we are all part of. To damage ones environment is in reality destroying our universe from the inside out. Society can choose to be either a cancer in the universe, or a positive healing force that will benefit everyone, including the conscious being that we all live in, and like to call GOD.

I know you're all saying New World Order right? Well let's think about it. What's so bad about a common belief and goal? Who wouldn't want a positive unity in Humanity? Evil people that's who, the fear of one world, is their work!!, chaos is the root of all evil. Evil lies in the mind within your doubt, and discontent. If we can understand who we are, then we can create a common reality of peace, and harmony. Only by doing this can we heal the planet we have been abusing.

We all have control of our personal surroundings by our choice of freewill and with determination for a better day tomorrow. Let's not let Evil scare us into believing unity is a bad thing. It is what is required to remove chaos from the world and universe. To progress in a fashion of our choosing and make life's journey a beautiful path again should be our common goal in our coexistence. I think most of us choose to have goodwill, if not affected by the distorted views of others.

A New World order does not have to be the beast stamped bar coded and mindless drone world it has been portrayed as in the propaganda, unless we let it be, by losing our freewill. I would prefer to think of the new world as a New World Accord, a global and individual agreement to respect each other, not only as another person of physical existence, but as another being of equal value and capable of intelligent thought. The more we disregard others opinions and ideas, the more we isolate our perspective limiting our vision to one of arrogance, and then ignorance due to our own ego. To be appreciated by others we must appreciate their existence. ~In Lak'ech ~<3~<3~<3~

About the Author

I am a simple man that has had more than my share of chaos in the world. I grew up in the world as I traveled through it. Starting at 9 years old, I was fortunate enough to visit other countries that my father worked in as a consultant and programmer while computers advanced. While visiting other countries, and experiencing new cultures as well as the different beliefs, I found a lot of different perspectives. Because I was a really good listener, and a little on the inquisitive, and quite side, I was constantly observing the world around me and learned a lot. I also had the pleasure of accompanying my mother and brother during the holidays while on vacations.

When I was 12 and living in Newport Beach, California, I had a Laser sailboat that I would cruise around the harbor in on sunny days, well make that any days with wind, I was in it a lot. One day, I was out by the mouth of the harbor and decided that the little island that I saw off in the distance was close enough to sail to. As I headed out in its direction the seas became very large for a 14ft craft and I began to get concerned. But, it wasn't until the waves were crashing over the bow instead or lapping around it, that I turned back. A good thing too, I later found out that the name of that island was Catalina, and it was 22 miles away, definitely not advisable for a child in a small sailboat. I guess we all have grand delusions when we are kids.

My life seems to have given me a very broad perspective of reality. After getting in some trouble for ditching school, I meet my first love. Then after taking the proficiency exam, and before moving to Westwood, and then Paso Robles, California, we traveled around the country on all kinds of road trips.

After a misunderstanding we parted ways, and I left to concentrate my efforts on making a living. I went on to make my way as a carpenter, and lather, which turned into a career in construction, primarily in metal framing, and electrical work. There were a lot of drywall hanging, and taping jobs in there too. I also had the pleasure of working on the Hamilton Cove project doing the framing, drywall, and some of the electrical work in the first couple phases. (This was on Catalina Isle. Coincidentally), while I was working there, I went in on the purchase of a boat for a place to live on the island. It was great fun for a while. Unfortunately it sank. =o(

If you're ever SCUBA Diving off the casino look for a 28' cabin cruiser called, the Loose Screw. Yea, I know, Bad choice in names right? But it wasn't my choice. LoL Anyway, after leaving the island, I got into Off-road racing rail-buggy's for a little while with Toyota of Escondido **(class 7).** After taking a second and third place in a couple of races, the firecracker 250 and the Parker 400, between 1983-85 I think it was. I had to return once again to work, and education. So I started at Devry, for electronics tech. Unfortunately, I didn't have the time, energy, or money to do both work full time construction, and go to school. So back to construction I went, progressing in both quality and speed, in the trades of carpentry, lath, electrical, concrete, taping, and T-bar, along with a touch of plumbing, and roofing, which I hated by the way. I found what I thought was love again after a while and had two wonderful boys. Unfortunately my wife and I had a difference of opinion in morals, so the marriage only lasted a couple years. After the divorce, I spent six months in Australia with some distant friends of the family for stress relief. I worked for them as skilled labor doing landscaping, and constructing brick driveways, pathways, and waterfalls.

I won't go into it but I really got the short end of the stick on the divorce considering that I was the faithful one. But that was years ago and society had different perspectives of what was best for the kids. Anyway, after returning to the Great United States, I returned to Sacramento and the trades to support myself and my kids, one of which lived with me a few months after my return.

After injuring my back on the job, and my mother passing away in 2006, I received some additional education in CADD drafting from the insurance company. Unfortunately, this was during our most recent recession, and there was no real work to be found as an inexperienced CADD drafter. So after the funds ran out, and I had to settle with the insurance company that denied my 3 level back surgery which happened to be recommended by the Dr. (Greedy little insurance companies).

Anyway, I had to seek other options. During this time, I meet another beautiful young lady that I fell in love with. This didn't last very long either due to the age difference or mental attitude, and perspective of honesty. I think she was still a little immature in her beliefs of reality, and this caused problems with her believing that her own perspective was the common reality. I know I should have known, but I wasn't my true self yet. Things were quite stressful and chaotic in my head. I believe that the realization of the purpose of life, may have had an effect on the way I perceive reality.

This inspired me and prompted me to work for myself again, to compensate for a lack of ability to wear my tool belt for 8 hrs at a time, and not having the full flexibility of my back as well. It was nice to work at my own pace anyway, I think that I actually made more money while the fun lasted, anyway, again things in the financial world of reality went downhill, and work slowed down.

During this time my ex-wife passed away also, giving me the pleasure of having both of my kids living with me at the same time. This was a difficult time for the family and prompted me to seek answers in truth and reality. In an effort to answer these questions, I ventured onto the internet or (**my personal key to the patent office**) as I like to call it. Through the internet, I gathered all the information that was available from the people of the world that wished to ask why. Thankfully there was YouTube with videos, and online dictionaries for reference. I seemed to learn, and understand extremely fast visually, and this aided me in formulating a realistic picture of how things worked, and why we are here. I seem to have a very visually creative mind. You could even say photographic at times in a way. Anyway, I did this by choice, and by the action and motion of flexing my freewill and determination to learn, there was really nothing else to do considering the depression and unemployment rate. It cost me nothing except my interest to find out as much as I could. And you know what? When you're interested in something, not only is a video priceless in explanation, but there are tons of them available for free. All you have to do is type in the subject of your interest, and filter through the rubbish. But, Lets' keep that a secret or someone will start trying to charge us for it. =o)

We are all capable of logically determining what's best for the world. We are capable of accepting a more effective perspective. We can do this by putting our priorities straight, relative to our common goals. Instead of an individual desire and quest, we need to desire a quest for peace, and compassion for everyone. Since we are all ultimately the same and part of each other anyway, it's the only logical thing to do.

The natural order of life is to create and coexist, Good and evil have perfect balance, it is the individual thoughts and actions that write the new page in our heart and souls records. The demons in our head are the hunger of our selfish greed. When we act selfishly this forms a habit of thinking in our perspective, unless our perspective is changed to a respectful and compassion thought process, we will find ourselves growing greedier, and never able to have enough in life, thus never content with what we have.

~ It's time to make a <u>Choice</u> and express you're Freewill,
Take action for the common good of all Humanity.

~ `Life is a Journey, enjoy the Path, But,
Don't Forget to Stop to Enjoy the Beauty `

~ Thanks for your interest in bettering the world.
Life can be wonderful for us all, All we have to do, is put
Forth the effort..

"To walk without looking is Ignorant,
Know where you're going, and make it happen."

"Only thru Goodwill and Determination,
Can we proceed forward in Life "

The Definition of God = Goodwill Over development

A thought entered my mind, It seems one must be, or appear a little crazy to visualize, and perceive life as it truly is. This as series of variable energy, light, sound waves, and frequencies, before they are deciphered by our mind, but then I think about humanity's perspectives, attitudes, and actions. And then I begin to question what we call sanity itself. Are we all crazy?

What have we been doing to ourselves and why? Who started the insane cycle of, I am the better person because, I have more stuff? Sure it's good to aspire for your goals, we all must. But we have forgotten to include the rest of humanity as our main purpose of improving life in the first place. The benefit of improving yourself comes when you can improve and benefit the life of society. We are all on the same journey with the same goal, a team working for the progress of humanity. When everyone is a ball hog, we lose the game by default. ~ Make a difference to those in your reach.

~ The Yin and Yang of life may pull us east and west. But the destination is always north in and along the winding trail. South takes us against our grain..

~ All things are as they should be at the moment, but the future isn't set for the day until we slumber that evening..~<3~

~ I/We are the current of life. I/We are equal to. Our determination, over the resistance of Humanity..   I = V/R

~ Life is what we make of it, your thoughts and actions are only limited to your freewill and determination in life.

~ As we walk the path of life, there are always footprints in the sand for us to follow, occasionally the trail becomes hard, and then we must have the freewill and determination to follow our knowledge and instinct until we reach the next plateau of surf and sand. enjoy and take note of the sea breeze, it can guide you through times of lost bearings, Like Alice in wonderland, we all have to discover whom we really are.

~ An arrogant and self-righteous perspective is all you need to fall from grace, without love and compassion we are left holding the bag of greed and envy. Being the victim of our own stupidity is our own fault because, It is only due to the circumstances and greed of our preference without consideration of the effect.

~ New knowledge should bring new lessons, repeating the old ones gets tiresome and depressing, not to mention redundant. Live today for tomorrow physically today is a gift, and tomorrow can always be missed, but whatever we learn helps us transform into better beings as we progress through the eternal foggy mist.

Which direction we go from here, depends entirely on...

YOU!!

Written by Bret Varcados ~ In Lak'ech ~<3~<3~<3~

Work Cited from and referenced to page

1) What the bleep? ~ Conceived by William Arntz

2) www.spaceandmotion.com/wave-structure-matter-theorists.htm

3) Wikipedia online encyclopedia ~ http://en.wikipedia.org/wiki/Cymatics

4) YouTube ~ http://www.youtube.com/videos?feature=mh

5) Glenn Wilson (2010)Born Gay?

The origins of sexual orientation. Information Retrieved from:
<http://foratv/2010/04/19/Glenn_wilson_born_gay_the_origins_of_sexual_orientation>